Jean Paton

CHICAGO TUMBLES

An account of events in the 1984-85 National Miners Strike, and it's impact on the Town of Cowdenbeath

First published March 1994 by Alex Maxwell.

Printed and bound in Great Britain by Barr Printers Glenrothes Ltd.

Front Cover Picture: Kenny Aitken

ISBN 0 9523230 0 1

Price £4.95

THE AUTHOR

Alex Maxwell was born in Airdrie, and came to Cowdenbeath in 1959 to take up a post in management in the Coal Board Workshops in Cowdenbeath, until made redundant in 1987. He worked part-time at Glasgow College of Commerce and Lauder College in Dunfermline, before becoming a full-time Lecturer in Trade Union Studies at Lauder, where he is also the E.I.S. Union convener. As part of his work he led the Mining Heritage Group in Benarty which produced the book 'No More Bings In Benarty' in 1992.

Alex was a Town Councillor in Cowdenbeath for ten years, stood for Parliament on four occasion, and was Chair of Cowdenbeath Community Council for ten years, being the architect of the Town's Centenary Celebrations in 1990.

He was elected as a Democratic Left Councillor to Dunfermline District Council in 1992 representing his adopted town, Cowdenbeath.

Acknowledgments.

I would like to thank all the many people who made this publication possible. In particular my wife Mary, who suffered the continual changes I made to the text as she put it on 'disc', to Les Cooney who collaborated with me on the draft and off whom I 'bounced' ideas. To Eddie Garvie who checked the authenticity of the facts, and to Jack Allan, who disputed them sometimes and put me right.

I am also indebted to the Dunfermline Press Management for the liberal use they allowed me of material from the Central Fife Times, and to the individuals who lent me photographs and written material.

Others who should be thanked are too numerous to mention, but their names are contained in the text and in the Roll of Honour at the end. Without them this book could never have been written.

Alex Maxwell
March 1994.

FOREWORD

Despite the fact that the 1984/85 Miners Strike was the longest and one of the most bitter industrial struggles in British History and its repercussions have been grave not just for the Coal Industry, but for the whole of the British people, remarkably little has been written in Scotland to tell the story of that Strike and the people involved. Therefore this book is very welcome.

With the massive Pit Closure programme since the Strike and the further dangers to the industry from Privatisation of what remains, the reality is that future generations will see little visible evidence of an industry which once employed $1{{1}\over{4}}$ million men and women. All over Scotland there are towns and villages which came into being only because of Coal, and almost every aspect of life was influenced by that Industry. When the pits closed, it was the end of a way of life, which had many positive features.

Cowdenbeath is such a town, built on mining, and I welcome the initiative taken by the author of this book to ensure that the events and characters involved in the Strike are recorded so that those who took part, and generations to come, will understand and appreciate what happened, what it meant, and its place in local history.

Today the Scottish Miners continue to campaign for a future for the Coal Industry in Scotland. We believe that the pits and the people who worked in them have been needlessly sacrificed in the interests of the giant Private Companies who dominate the Energy Industry. Indeed as part of that campaign I led a group of miners on a 630 mile march from Scotland through the English Coalfields to London to highlight the Case for Coal. It was a particular pleasure to be given a Civic Reception in Cowdenbeath prior to our departure, when I met again many of our former colleagues from the days of the Strike.

Whatever the final outcome of that campaign we recognise that the 1984/85 Strike was of critical importance to our Mining Industry and a major historic event in Britain. Certainly it will be remembered for the courage and endurance of those mining families, their loyalty to their union, and that Community spirit which characterises Mining Areas.

However, this book tells not only of the events and characters involved in Cowdenbeath during the Strike, it comments on how it was conducted nationally and locally, it's positive and negative features, it's consequences for the Coal Industry, as well as for the town of Cowdenbeath, and reflects on the lessons so bitterly learned for us all in the Trade Union movement. In writing it Alex Maxwell has added not just a new chapter to Local History but has contributed to the continuing debate about the future of the Coal Industry in Britain.

George Bolton
President – NUM Scottish Area

CONTENTS

INTRODUCTION		9
CHAPTER 1	Understanding the Miner – the Historical Background	13
CHAPTER 2	Chicago Born	19
CHAPTER 3	Cowdenbeath Workshops	31
CHAPTER 4	In The Beginning	37
CHAPTER 5	Chronology of the Strike	47
CHAPTER 6	Running the Strike and Struggling to Survive	59
CHAPTER 7	It's a Miracle No One was Killed	73
CHAPTER 8	Actions Incompatible with My Position	85
CHAPTER 9	Whit Did ye' Dae in the Strike, Mum?	95
CHAPTER 10	Battling for the Hearts and Minds	109
CHAPTER 11	Scabs, Super-Scabs and Others who Returned	137
CHAPTER 12	The End and Afterwards	149
CHAPTER 13	Was it all Worthwhile?	159
CHAPTER 14	Ten Years On – Personal Reflections	169
	The Roll of Honour	181

INTRODUCTION

"Without doubt Cowdenbeath is the Chicago of Fife" proclaimed Bailie James Laing in a moment of great exuberance at a Town Council Meeting 100 years ago. Looking at Cowdenbeath today it would be difficult to envisage any parallel at all between this small Fife town (pop. 10,500) and that great industrial city in Illinois, U.S.A.

To those of us brought up in the golden years of American gangster movies, featuring Cagney, Bogart, Edward G Robinson and the other silver screen heroes, it is impossible to imagine that Cowdenbeath was ever the scene of bootleggers, mobsters, racketeers and crime with it's own home-grown Al Capones - and indeed it never was.

The reason for Bailie Laing's statement was of course more simple. He was living in a time when Cowdenbeath was developing rapidly, the population multiplying, new houses and businesses springing up everywhere, and it was this rapid expansion which prompted him to make the comparison.

Laing, himself had a Grocer's shop on the High Street, and in the same speech went on to declare that this Town's main thoroughfare *"would soon resemble Princes Street in Edinburgh"*. Whilst anyone examining the Town today, despite the brave attempts to improve it's appearance, must wonder how such grandiose statements could ever have been made in the first place, there was indeed some justification for the Bailie's elation.

By comparison with neighbouring towns like Dunfermline, Inverkeithing, Burntisland and even Lochgelly, Cowdenbeath is comparatively young, emerging as an important coal mining centre, just over 100 years ago. It was the discovery of coal which gave birth to the town of Cowdenbeath - indeed it was it's sole reason for being. It was coal mining that dominated every aspect of life in the town and determined its destiny.

A study of the history of coal mining and the miners over 150 years in this area will show that it is one littered with countless Strikes, local and national, as miners fought constantly to try and maintain employment, reasonable wages and conditions at work, and a decent quality of life in their communities, against ruthless coal owners. However, ironically, the longest ever strike of miners in this Country took place in 1984 when the industry was in public ownership, with consequences that have been devastating for mining communities.

I should say that when I started to gather the material for this book, my intention was purely to record events of the Strike as they related to Cowdenbeath, who was involved, and the impact on the Community at large, something which had been neglected by those who had taken part in the great struggles of the Miners Lock-out in 1921 and the General Strike of 1926.

Perhaps it could be claimed that the miners were *"too busy making history, to record it"* but nevertheless it is a major gap in our local history that little has been written about those momentous times for future generations to study.

Therefore I had resolved that this would not happen this time, and so in the aftermath of the 1984/85 strike, I set about collecting as much information as I could accumulate. For that I am indebted to the NUM Branch Officials, the members of the Cowdenbeath Strike Committee and the Womens Support Group for the minutes of their meetings and other records loaned to me, and for the co-operation of the individuals who shared their thoughts and experiences with me in taped recordings. In addition I gathered all the written publications issued by the Miners Unions and extracted every article I could about the Strike from the local and national newspapers.

In writing this account I also had an advantage over any other author I know of. I was employed in Management in the Coal Board at Cowdenbeath Workshops during the Strike, except for the three months I was suspended from duty for publicly supporting the Miners, and at the same time I was in close contact with all of the strikers activities and doing as much possible to help their cause.

Whilst readers should appreciate the frustrations of my position neverthe-

INTRODUCTION

less I am better able to describe from personal knowledge the local tactics being employed on both sides in the dispute. In addition I had three sons who were on strike the whole year, which gave me some insight of the effects of the strike on members of my own family. Consequently I felt well equipped for my task. Unfortunately despite my good intentions and for no justifiable reason I failed at the time to complete the book I set out to produce.

Two events since however, stirred my conscience. First the town of Cowdenbeath celebrated it's centenary as a Burgh, and as a result of my deep involvement in the commemorative events I came to realise that the 1984/85 Miners Strike was of even greater significance to the town than I had appreciated at the time.

Then I became involved through my work as a tutor at Lauder College in Dunfermline, with a group of retired people who formed the Benarty Mining Heritage Group, and decided to record the rise and fall of mining in that part of Fife.

This led to the production of a book, "No More Bings in Benarty" for which along with a college student Les Cooney, I collated and edited the material, and indeed wrote a fair bit of it myself. The book was a huge local success and made me determined to go back to my earlier pledge on the Cowdenbeath book, about the Strike.

During the course of writing this book I changed my mind from time to time about what form it should take. I finally decided it should set the Strike within the whole history of mining in this area, it should describe what happened and who was involved, it should contain individual experiences and opinions, and I would include my own memories of what happened at the time and reflections on the consequences.

Looking back after ten years what is now abundantly evident is that the 1984/85 Miners Strike, apart from the disastrous consequences for the British Miners, was the last great national strike we will ever witness in the coal industry. As far as Cowdenbeath is concerned it effectively ended any connection the town had with coal mining. The industry which gave birth to the town just over 100 years has gone, and with it Cowdenbeath's original reason for being!

The *'Chicago of Fife'* had finally been humbled, tumbling far from it's eminent past, and the claims of Bailie Laing. Hence my title 'Chicago Tumbles' of a book which describes that epic 12 months fight and failure to retain the remains of coal mining - in the longest and most bitter struggle of all the struggles the mining families endured in the lifetime of this town.

Certainly for those who took part in the Strike it was an episode in their lives that they could never forget, and their personal memories of those days will be handed down to succeeding generations. I hope they feel my efforts although often clearly a personal view of the Strike, are worthy of the hardships they suffered and the sacrifices they made during that titanic battle, because all of them have my deepest respect and lasting admiration.

But I also hope that this book will be, for future generations, a useful reference in their study of Mining Heritage. Whilst the focal point of my work has been the town of Cowdenbeath, I am sure it has a wider audience and will strike a chord with many people whose own roots are to be found in former mining communities through Britain.

CHAPTER 1

UNDERSTANDING THE MINER - THE HISTORICAL BACKGROUND

When the year-long Miners Strike finally ended on the 5th March 1985, with the return to work 'without a settlement' 85% of those who had walked out of the Cowdenbeath Workshops a year before had remained on strike throughout the entire period. This was typical of the situation throughout the Fife Coalfield.

Despite all the pressures of poverty and hardship, the arrests, fines and subsequent dismissal of pickets, the massive media campaign of the Government and the National Coal Board, designed to demoralise and weaken the resolve of the striking miners, and even although the strike has collapsed in Ayrshire and the Lothians, the fact was that the overwhelming majority of the Fife Miners remained loyal to their union and to their fellows. The struggle was carried on to the bitter end.

It was a situation that had perplexed the Coal Board management in Scotland who had spent massive sums of money on Press adverts and on propaganda sent direct to the men's homes, offering ever new 'inducements' to try and break the solidarity of those still holding fast.

To people who know little about the nature of coalmining and the history of the miners it is difficult to understand why, in spite of the growing inevitability of defeat, the Fife miners in the main refused to succumb to the pressures from the government and the Coal Board.

THE ROOTS OF MILITANCY

The answers become clearer, however by an appreciation of the history of the Fife Miners, and the roots of their militant tradition, particularly in Cowdenbeath, the focus of our attention.

Cowdenbeath's connection with coal is reputed to have begun 2000 years ago, when the Romans, whose army of occupation used coal for heating purposes, fought a battle with the Caledonians near Leuchatsbeath to the north of the town.

However, coal is not actually mentioned in early history in Fife until the 13th Century when the monks at Dunfermline Abbey established workings in the lands around the Pittencrieff area, but only mining sufficient coal for their own heating needs, with any surplus going to the local peasantry.

The Fife coal industry really developed in the latter part of the sixteenth century when Sir George Bruce mined the coal in large quantities at Culross, for both the production of salt and for export to Europe.

From that time the output of coal rose steadily as it became a major source of energy for newly expanding industries, and when King James V1 ascended the throne and looked across his Kingdom from his palace at Falkland at the curling smoke of the coal mines he could justifiably describe his Kingdom as a 'beggar's mantle with a fringe of gold'.

But if coal was a vital part of the Scottish economy it needed people to mine it, and to put it mildly it was not exactly the most attractive job in the world. Indeed it was almost impossible to get volunteers, and the Government introduced laws which compelled 'vagrants' (there were thousands of them at the time) and their children to bondage in the mines.

By an Act of Parliament in 1606

> *(i) No one could hire a collier, coal bearer or salter without his master's permission.*
>
> *(ii) If any collier, coal bearer or salter left their employment without permission, his master has the right to reclaim him.*
>
> *(iii) His new master would be forced to surrender him within 24 hours, under penalty of a fine of £100, Scots, for each time of asking.*
>
> *(iv) Any deserting collier, coal bearer or salter would be deemed a thief,*

and punished accordingly.

(v) Powers were given to masters and owners of coal-heughs to apprehend all vagabonds and beggars and put them to work.

In effect miners had become slaves - they were cut off from the rest of their fellow men, tied to the mine where they worked and sold almost as part of the equipment. Their children were forced down the pit at eight years old, working from 16 to 18 hours and wives and daughters were used as human beasts of burden to carry coal to the surface.

And the miners were not only treated as slaves at work, by their employers. They were regarded by other working people as little more than vagabonds, and even in death not allowed the same rights as the poorest of their neighbours. Indeed in Fife well into the 19th century they were not allowed to be buried in the same graveyard as other more 'respectable folk'.

NO LONGER SLAVES - BUT STILL SHACKLED

The final ending of slavery for the miners in 1799, whilst very welcome, did not just come about by a concern by the government for democratic freedoms. The growing demand for coal to satisfy the energy needs of the Industrial Revolution could not be met by workmen who had no incentive to work - serfdom became a barrier to the growth of production and had to go.

However, the newly-freed miners rights were severely controlled as the British Government, alarmed by the recent French Revolution, took steps to ensure there was no repeat here. A series of 'Combination Acts' were introduced forbidding workers from 'combining' together to better their conditions - the first anti-Trade Unions laws in effect.

In a period when a massive expansion of the coal industry was taking place and huge profits being made by the coal owners, the 'Masters' were making sure the workers could not take concerted action to share their wealth.

Nevertheless despite these repressive laws, discontent at the harsh conditions and low wages resulted in the growth of numerous 'underground societies' and at a time when the Chartist Movement was campaigning for political reform, Trade Unions began to appear, and with the repeal of the hated Combination Laws in 1824, the first of these in the coal industry emerged, initially as single pit unions and then as 'County' unions.

Part of the development of the 'County' unions taking place in the mid 19th century was the formation of the Fife and Kinross Miners Association in 1870. It was in that year of the Franco- Prussian war when the demand for coal was at a premium, the struggle to reduce the working day to eight hours took place, and as a result of bold and united action the Fife miners became the first in Europe to win the eight hour day, an outcome which labelled the Fife men as the 'most militant' in Britain.

If it was a reputation not entirely deserved at that time as they had been indeed for a long time more moderate in their political outlook than miners elsewhere, then their subsequent history more than fully justified it.

Incidentally the winning of the 8-hour day by the Fife miners was celebrated by the establishment of a Gala Day held on the first Saturday in June 1871 when 2000 miners and their families along with seven bands gathered in Kirkcaldy for a day of races, games and dancing on the shore.

Over the next few years as wages and conditions improved, miners flocked into the Union, and Fife became the strongest of the County Unions. Then another of the cyclical slumps hit the coal industry, and a series of wages cuts took place resulting in strikes in which the miners were defeated. Whilst union strength in Scotland as a whole was severely weakened, in Fife the County Union was still able to maintain it's footing.

As the economic crisis deepened in early 1877 the coal masters proposed a further cut of 10% in already low wages. The Fife miners resisted and were 'locked-out' to enforce the reduction. The result was a 14-week long strike which ended in a substantial victory for the men. This victory was a landmark in the history of the Scottish miners, for defeat of their strongest County Union could have meant the end of effective union organisation in Scotland.

The great economic crisis from 1877 and reaching it's depths in 1879, had serious effects on the miners unions in Scotland. Wages were cut, victimisation was rife, in locality after locality union organisation was destroyed or went under-ground and by 1880 only the Fife and Kinross Miners

Association was left.

There was some revival in the next few years but up to 1894 only the Fife organisation could be called a really established union. In that year at a time when the Scottish coal trade was much better than in England, where miners were on short-time, the employers sought to impose a further reduction in already low wages.

This produced the first ever all-Scottish strike, to which the coal owners reacted by invoking the forces of law on their behalf in order to crush the miners, leading to unprecedented police brutality on pickets at the collieries. After 10 weeks of great hardship the strike began to crack, and some 20% of the original 70,000 miners were 'blacklegging'. In the event the strike in the rest of Scotland lasted fifteen weeks, but again Fife miners carried on a further fortnight, enhancing their 'most militant' image.

Over the next 18 years the ebb and flow of wages continued, in line with the state of the coal trade, but the election of a Liberal Government, with the advent of 29 Labour MP's brought about not only the welcome Trade Dispute Act, but also the Eight Hour Act for Miners. The initial feeling that major advances would be won through Parliament, however, was soon dissipated as Labour was clearly not yet capable of challenging the two main capitalist parties in Parliament. The miners concluded that they would need national union action to achieve justice in their industry.

A series of national conferences laid the basis for concerted action and armed with substantial victories in strike ballots throughout the coalfields, the claim for a National Minimum Wage was lodged with the employers. Government intervention failed to resolve the situation and on Friday 1st March 1912 a strange silence fell in the coalfields. No seams were being worked underground in Britain and no coal was being wound to the surface. For the first time in seven hundred years there was an utter cessation of work in the mining industry.

The great National Minimum Wage Strike had begun, the first ever National Strike in Britain's Coal Industry. It lasted six weeks, but whilst it resulted in the passing of a Minimum Wage Bill through Parliament, it was to prove only a partial victory.

It's real significance was it demonstrated for the first time that the men who manned the pits could, organise themselves nationally to fight successfully for better wages and conditions.

It was an experience repeated on a number of occasions over the next seventy years in a sequence of national strikes, culminating with what, in my view, would prove to the the last great national strike of all in 1984/85 which had disastrous consequences for the coal industry, the miners, and the mining communities, from which they have never recovered.

CHAPTER 2

CHICAGO BORN

As I intend to deal specifically with the town of Cowdenbeath in the context of the 1984/85 Strike, it is necessary to identify where that town fitted into the picture I have painted so far of the Fife miners in the latter part of the 19th Century and the beginning of the 20th Century.

Up till the advent of the 19th Century Cowdenbeath had been an agricultural area in decline, made up of a series of crofts and farms, The discovery of coal at Kelty revived it's fortunes somewhat, but it really took off in 1850 when the Oakley Iron Company insearch of iron ore, stumbled instead across rich seams of coal. Following this discovery and as iron ore became less profitable, pits were sunk in every corner of the area, and a rapid expansion of the town began.

Subject of course to the recurring booms and slumps in the demand for Coal I have outlined the town developed as an important centre of the mining industry in Scotland, enhanced by the construction of the railway to Perth and the conquering of the river Forth by a massive rail bridge. By 1890 it had grown to the degree that demand for the elementary services of water, sanitation, roads, and lighting became irresistible and it's leading citizens launched a campaign to secure Burgh status for the town.

This was granted by the Sheriff of Fife on 24 November 1890, and in the subsequent elections in Brunton's Hall (now located in the Cowdenbeath Business Centre) Henry Mungall the Chairman of the Cowdenbeath Coal Company topped the poll with 244 votes and became the first Provost of the town. Considering the population of the town a the time was over 3,000 and even as the election took place thousands of local miners were on strike against his Coal Company, Mungall's victory might seem a contradition. However unusual that may seem now, it is important to remember that the majority of miners had no vote at that time and of course the women had no vote at all!

So the Chairman of the local Coal company became the Civic Head of the Town, a town which was growing so rapidly it's population was doubling every ten year, and developing at such a rate as to produce from a leading figure in the town, Baillie James Laing that legendary description of the '*Chicago of Fife*'.

Mungall, the new Provost, went on in his career to become the Chairman of the Fife Coal Company, one of the most progressive mining companies of it's time, if at the same time one of the most ruthless in it's drive for profit. It is significant that even in the worst days in the coal trade it continued to make a profit and pay dividends, and its shares had a greater value than all it's competitors. Few would question the engineering ability and foresight of those who were to lead that company over the next 50 years.

It was their humanity which was lacking in their relations with those who made their wealth.

Incidentally it says a lot about the history and nature of Cowdenbeath that the first Provost of the town was the representative of the hated coal owners, whilst the last Provost in 1974 was a Communist - Willie Sharp, a former miner at Bowhill Colliery. Old Henry must have turned in his grave at the time!

However to illustrate the relations between miners and 'masters' locally, in the same year that Mungall became Provost of Cowdenbeath, the threat of yet another strike prompted the Cowdenbeath Coal Company to act against the would-be strikers by taking the hitherto unheard of step of withdrawing the supply of domestic coal to the miners' homes. In an article on the action, the Dunfermline Journal commented critically that '*no other coal owner had taken such a step*' and that the Cowdenbeath Coal Company '*has got famed for this bit of would be sharp practice*'.

The 'sharp practice' of course meant that by stopping the delivery of fire coal the Company were attacking not just the miner, but his wife and family, already living in the discomfort of the 'Company house'. Whilst the miner was technically free, nevertheless the Company controlled his life. He lived in a Company house, and had to abide by Company rules and conditions. Evictions were commonplace, especially during lock-outs and strikes and once black-listed a miner would find it almost impossible to find work at his trade in the district.

The houses themselves of course reflected the concern that the coal owners had for the welfare of their employees and their families - very little! The 'miners rows' were a national scandal. Large families crammed into the traditional 'but and ben', stone floors, damp walls, leaky roofs, a 'dry closet' outside as a shared toilet, water drawn from the street well, ramshackle wash-houses, the 'privvy midden' for ashes and refuse. Cooking was often done on an open fire. Coal and explosives were stored under the kitchen bed, as was the family washtub which was hauled out to the centre of the floor when the occupants washes themselves.

The miners wives did their best to make their homes hospitable, scrubbing and polishing, but for many their lives were a continual drudgery, with not even the temporary escape to one of the numerous local drinking houses where their husbands sought solace and company.

MOSS-MORRAN DISASTER

In their drive for greater profits the coal-owners had little regard for the safety of the men and women who worked for them - they could be easily replaced from the ranks of the unemployed. On average 1000 men a year died in Britain's pits at the turn of the century, with a further 130,000 suffering serious injury.

A family who depended on the householders earnings would quickly find themselves in dire straits if the breadwinner was injured at work and forced to *'lie off'* with no money coming in. Compensation for industrial injuries was minimal, and in the all too common instance of a fatality, the victim's family had to settle for a mere pittance. Locally never a week went by without a report of some injury or death in the Cowdenbeath Collieries.

The year 1901 was a particularly disastrous one for the Cowdenbeath area, when in two separate incidents, at Hill of Beath and Donibristle, 15 men lost their lives. At the Hill of Beath engine Pit seven were overcome and died of gas poisoning, and at Donibristle No 12 Pit eight more perished underground. In the latter case men had been trapped by an inrush of liquid moss as they attempted to drive an outlet to the surface, and between them and the valiant miners who tried to rescue them, the lives of George Hutchison, Alex Smith, William Forsyth, David Campbell, Willliam Hynd, James McDonald, Thomas Rattray, Andrew Paterson were lost.

Because vast profits were being made at the time due to the demand for coal, and consequently coal owners were prepared to take risks, there were many who questioned the way the accident had happened and whether the Fife Coal Company had been negligent.

A local poet James Murray put these sentiments into verse and sold his poems to raise funds for the widows of the dead miners.

> "Was it an accident, or was it neglect?
> Well perhaps it is hard now to say
> But we all know the men lost their lives
> While toiling for five bob a day.
> Was that all their poor lives were worth
> Was it enough to keep want from the door?
> Well our masters they don't give a snuff
> They swear they can't pay any more"

In his report of the disaster HM Inspector of Mines J.B. Atkinson said that 'this accident shows plainly the danger of tapping moss from below and that in making a connection between the surface and workings beneath such material (moss) the work should be prosecuted downwards and not upwards'
It is only of late that coal has been worked on a large scale under moorland, and this incident is a valuable lesson to many mines now working under mosses'

Whilst the report then resulted in laying down minimum thicknesses between moss and underground workings, the lesson was in fact not learnt and fifty years later under the control of the National Coal Board an inrush of moss at Knockshinnock in Ayrshire cost the lives of several men.

At the subsequent enquiry Scottish Miners President Abe Moffat in a most competent presentation and drawing on the report of the Mossmorran disaster laid the blame squarely on the shoulders of the Coal Board, maintaining that the accident should have been prevented and had only occurred due to breaches of the Coal Mines Act by those responsible for it's enforcement.

Giving credence to the miners feelings at nationalisation that those who now controlled the industry were *'the same team in different jerseys'*, Moffat said in his submission that *'more than once the criticism was heard that the N.C.B's attitude was little different from that of the colliery owners, who always sought to show that no blame could possibly be attached to their officials nor themselves. The Coal Board was more concerned to avoid the risks of actions for Common Law damages"*

And when it came to paying decent compensation to the families of those who lost their lives at Knockshinnock, the same miserly attitude was adopted by the Coal Board initially until forced to acknowledge their responsibilities to the dependents. Truly old habits died hard!

THE COMMON BOND

In examining all the reasons why the Fife mining communities reacted in the way they did in the 1984/85 Strike, the historical background of the miners I described earlier is important. From the period of slavery when they were treated almost as subhuman and set apart from the rest of society, they moved into a way of life that was still controlled by their masters. They lived in the shadow of the pit bing in mining villages, in houses owned by the Company. In their relations with their employer they were all subject to the same exploitation, the same ruthless treatment, occupied the same 'miners rows' under the same primitive conditions.

The nature of their work down the pit, toiling in terrible conditions, subject to poisonous gases and roof-falls, with danger ever around the corner, demanded that they must rely on each other for their common safety and well-being and when disaster struck and men were entombed (as at Mossmorran in 1901) there was no shortage of volunteers to risk their lives to save those of their fellows.

The fact was that they were all in the same boat, and it was natural that the bond between them created by conditions of work underground was transferred and re-inforced on the surface above, in their 'miners rows'

This history and these conditions engendered that special community spirit which characterised mining areas, so that in time of industrial struggle there was unity of purpose, and in time of personal difficulty there was always a neighbour to give a helping hand, or a word of comfort to alleviate distress.

They shared a common bond, understanding that the survival of the individual family virtually depended on the survival of their community, and an injury to one was an injury to all. The Trade Union slogan that 'Unity is Strength' had a special meaning among miners and those who broke that unity and 'black-legged' during a dispute committed the unpardonable sin, and became outcasts by betraying the community.

Miners were a distinctive breed by the very nature of their work, and the lives of mining families were completely bound up with the fate of the coal industry. It was not just another way of earning a living - it was a whole way of life. And in Cowdenbeath it was the discovery of coal, the nature of the work and the fluctuating fortunes of the coal industry which shaped every aspect of life there creating those specific social, cultural and political features which distinguish the town and help us to evaluate the events there during the 1984/85 Miners Strike.

THE POLITICAL DIMENSION

Having looked earlier at some historical aspects of Trade Union struggle in Fife, it is also valuable to consider the political ingredients which consolidated the militancy that characterised the Fife Miners, and gave Fife it's special place in working class legend, with Cowdenbeath as our main interest.

The first National Miners Strikes of 1912 was followed by the first Great World War, in which millions of men on both sides lost their lives, virtually wiping out a generation. Finally having fought themselves to a standstill and weary at the futility of it all, the war ended and the troops trudged home, to the promise of a 'land fit for heroes'

But is was not to be. The times which followed were known as 'the revolutionary years' Whilst the only successful revolution was in Russia, nevertheless all over Europe there were great movements reacting against the horror of war and seeking change, not least here in Scotland. Men who had gone to war in a wave of patriotic fervour (including incidentally my own father) returned as rebels not prepared to meekly return to the conditions of the past.

The demands grew for better wages and conditions, decent housing and social services, and the miners were in the forefront of this movement. The Miners Union grew rapidly and so did the political parties of the Left. In the latter years of the War there had been a great anti-war movement and revolutionary ideas abounded, especially here in Fife. There were numerous strikes and demonstration against hunger and evictions and much Socialist agitation.

The Labour Party was winning mass support, the Independent Labour Party had considerable influence and the Communist Party was being born.

During the war there had been a tremendous demand for coal, and relations between the coal-owners and the miners had been easier. However, the end of the war brought about mass unemployment and a slump in the coal industry. The miners sought to improve wages to catch up with a large increase in the cost of living over the war years. After a two week strike the Government temporarily defused the situation, by linking wages to output, but then less than a year later asked the miners to accept an agreement which would cut their wages by almost 25%. The miners refused and were 'locked-out' of their pits by the coalowners.

THE 1921 LOCKOUT

All over Fife there were huge demonstrations in protest, the police moved in to guard the pits and the military were put on alert. On 4 April 1921 a mass rally of miners was held in the Empire Theatre (later to become the Cowdenbeath Palais) and from there they marched to Kirkford behind the Hill of Beath Pipe Band.

From Kirkford they saw smoke coming from the chimney of Dalbeath Pit and they promptly made their way there to find the colliery manager, Robert Gillespie, coal inspector George Christie and William Spalding, the colliery agent firing the boilers to keep the pumping machinery going. Grabbing hold of Spalding the miners threatened to throw him in the pit pond, then decided to carry him shoulder high down the road, resisted the calls to throw him in the Bleachfield Pond, went down the High Street and ended up at Union Street where they held a meeting. Up till then there had been an element of fun and good humour about the proceedings - although I doubt if the hapless Willie Spalding would see the joke - but the intervention of the police changed that.

The police charged the crowd, and rescued Spalding whom they put on a tram car going away from the scene. Police batons were used and the crowd replied with stones. In the confrontation policemen were injured and one miner, by name William Easton was arrested. A period of uneasy peace followed until 10.00pm when the crowd moved up the High Street. The police again made a baton charge sweeping down the street felling everyone who stood in their way, and cleared the area. The crowd regrouped later, but with all the lights turned out simultaneously the police once again swept up the High Street, and the crowd melted into the night.

The next day William Easton was brought before the Sheriff at Dunfermline and committed to prison for assaulting the police. These events in Cowdenbeath made the national headlines and the press related scare stories of 'extremists' and plots to overthrown the established order.

Indeed in later years when the Cabinet papers of that time were released it was revealed that there was serious concern at Government level that a Russian style revolution was about to break in Cowdenbeath. That was of course nonsense but the action of the authorities suggested that indeed they were alarmed.

COWDENBEATH UNDER MARTIAL LAW

After a week of comparative quiet in Cowdenbeath, on Wednesday 13 April 1921 *"Cowdenbeath ratepayers woke up to find that the burgh had been converted into what was virtually an armed camp"* (Dunfermline Press). In the early morning bus loads of solders and marines poured into the town, and military guards were installed at every pit-head. The soldiers were billeted in the Cairns Church, and the quiet efficiency with which the 'mid-night flit' was conducted could well be explained by the fact that Carlow Reid, the much-resented Chairman of the Fife Coal Company, was an elder of, and a substantial contributor to that church.

The same evening the Fife County police arrested a further eight men in connection with the events the week before and they were taken by motor char-a-banc to Dunfermline where they sang the *'Red Flag'* on their way to the cells in the Sheriff Court house.

All the men- Mick Moran, James McGinn, Archie Guthrie, David Savage, Robert Gear, James Spowart, John Whyte, John Kent and William Easton were subsequently tried at Perth High Court found guilty and sentenced to imprisonment, with Whyte, Kent and Easton being jailed for one year.

This incident in Cowdenbeath and the sentences dished out to the ringleaders had a profound impact on the political consciousness of the miners in the area. After 3 months on strike the miners were forced to return, defeated, but by now there were a new group of younger, more ardent Socialists who had emerged to challenge the leadership of the older union officials, some of them cradled in the Liberal tradition that had prevailed in Fife for many years.

The consequence was the formation of the Reform Union in 1922, which stiffened and led the resistance to the coalowners who, emboldened by the miners defeat in the strike increased the attack on their wages and working conditions. It's leadership was in the main drawn from active members of the Communist Party and this Communist influence amongst the miners was to increase steadily by their constant activity and agitation in the coalfields, through their role in the General Strike of 1926 and the years after, encompassing the Hungry Thirties.

These developments in the Miners Union are well documented elsewhere (R. Page Arnotts *'History of the Scottish Miners'*) and need not be expanded on here. Suffice to say that eventually the dominating people in the leadership of the Scottish District of the NUM were Communists with first Abe Moffat from Lumphinnans and then his brother Alex becoming Presidents, supported by many Communist miners agents and pit delegates in the coalfields, especially in Fife.

Parallel to this process in the Miners Union, through the 20's and 30's following the defeat of the miners in the 1926 strike was a rapid growth in membership of the Communist Party, whose leading figures were building up support in the villages and towns of West Fife by constant agitation and activity, organising the unemployed, fighting the Means Test, leading the Hunger Marches, opposing evictions, and campaigning for relief measures for the poverty stricken thousands of people with no work and little income.

Each Community had it's own leading figures - the Moffats in Lumphinnans and Glencraig, Jimmy Stewart in Lochgelly and in Cowdenbeath the legendary Bob Selkirk whose all too short personal history - *'The Life of a Worker'*- describes the events and nature of that significant background to the unique political character of this area, which led to the election of the first Communist M.P. in Britain - Willie Gallacher for West Fife in 1935 and in the same year the election of Bob Selkirk and David Fairley as Communist Councillors in Cowdenbeath.

It was in this period after the 1921 Strike, through the 1926 General Strike, and into the Hungry Thirties that the political dimension was being added to Fife's traditional militant reputation, and indeed confirming that reputation as being warranted.

Whilst in the electoral field support for Communist candidates declined in the intensity of the 'cold war' with Gallacher losing his Parliamentary seat in 1951 and most of the Councillors suffering the same fate, the Communist dominance of the Miners Union in Scotland was sustained, and the local pits by and large elected Communist officials to represent the miners.

Although Labour dominated the electoral arena the Communists still had the industrial support. However in Cowdenbeath, Communist Councillors continued to be elected with Selkirk and Willie Sharp representing Ward Four (known as 'owre the brig') in a Council controlled normally by Labour, although being lost on occasion to the 'Ratepayers' due to the complacency and arrogance which grew as a feature of Labour's single-party control over a long period.

There was a revival in support for the Communists in West Fife in the Sixties and early Seventies, and indeed in 1973, the year after a successful national miners strike, there were twelve Communist Councillors in the area between Ballingry and Cowdenbeath.

I had been elected to the Cowdenbeath Town Council in 1964, and although by 1973 the legendary 'Old Bob Selkirk' had retired, the town had four Communist Councillors, with the election of Tom Young, and 'Young Bob Selkirk' to join Willie Sharp and myself, amassing one-third of the popular vote.

To crown it all Cowdenbeath hit the national headlines as the first town ever in Britain to have a Communist Provost, Willie Sharp, a fitting reward for many years of devoted service to the townsfolk. Certainly this event underlined the fact that there was something special, indeed unique, about Cowdenbeath.

However this Communist triumph was short lived, and in the euphoria of another victorious national miners strike in 1974, and the fall of the Heath Government, Labour swept to power in Westminster. At virtually the same time Cowdenbeath Town Council was a victim of Local Government Reorganisation and in the subsequent Regional and District Council elections, every seat in West Fife, with the exception of Willie Clarke in Ballingry was lost.

In my own case the old Cowdenbeath Ward 4 had the village of Graypark added to make up the District seat, and I lost by a handful of votes to the Labour candidate Michael Judge. However in the next three elections, the margin between Labour and Communist remained close and it was clear that there was still considerable support for the Communist Party and its ideas in the town, based on its historical role, up till the 1984 Miners Strike. Given the historical mining traditions of Cowdenbeath and the unusual political background I have described it was only to be expected that the Strike would get wide support from the townspeople - and so it proved to be.

CHAPTER 3

COWDENBEATH WORKSHOPS

By the time of the 1984 Miners Strike, there were no longer any collieries in the area around Cowdenbeath. A town which lay in the heart of a coalfield in 1921 with 25 pits within a radius of 3 miles, no longer had a single colliery within 10 miles. The last pit in the town had gone in the programme of pit closures from 1955-1961. The remaining Coal Board establishment was the Cowdenbeath Central Workshops, which had been set up in 1925 by the Fife Coal Company.

This Coal Company had been one of the more progressive private concerns in Scotland, and with the development of mechanisation within its pits its owners realised the need for a central repair depot. The Workshops was created therefore just before the 1926 General Strike, and following the defeat on the miners the Coal Company carried out a policy of victimisation and discrimination against militants.

Consequently, the employees at the workshops were recruited from the families of the local middle class, shopkeepers, contractors, gaffers and 'trusties'. Membership of the local Masonic Lodge was said to be a prime qualification for a job there. In those days, as Mary Docherty, a veteran woman activist in Cowdenbeath, described it to me *'it was a place full of scabs and belly crawlers'*, and although that description maybe extreme, never-the-less quite clearly at the Workshops, there was no room for Communists or militant Trade Unionists.

The plant was ruled with a rod of iron and men could be sacked on the least excuse - for example there were no tea breaks, smoking was prohibited, and even visits to the toilets were timed to make sure there was no malingering. It was regarded locally as a 'prison camp'.

However, the outbreak of the 2nd World War began to change the picture. For the first time many militants who had been victimised during the 20's and 30's found work, as every able-bodied worker was needed to help the war effort. This opened the doors of the Workshops to a number of people who would not have previously been employed there, including for the first time, women workers, but only for the duration of the war.

With the end of the war being followed by nationalisation, this wider recruitment from the families of miners continued and indeed even a founder member of the Communist Party, Peter Venters, found a job there driving the machine shop crane.

However, when I arrived at the Workshops, in 1960, there was only one Communist who worked in the place, David Selkirk, the son of the famous Councillor, Bob Selkirk, but I met within the Workshops, a number of people such as Eddie Garvie and John Hynd from mining backgrounds in Kelty who I persuaded to become members of the Communist Party, as I was.

In 1962, in the Coal Board contraction programme of that time they decided to close the Workshops, as being surplus to their needs, but a massive public campaign which united not only the management and workers within the factory, but drew in the whole of the local community, forced the Coal Board to change their policy and the Workshops future was secured. This had been the first mass action to have taken place at the Workshops, throughout its history.

It was led by Labour militants and Communists (including myself) and its success strengthened the Trade Unions within the Factory. Indeed it was in this period, that the Workshops had its first ever strike, when the delegate of SCEBTA, (the Craftsmen's Union) the newly recruited Communist John Hynd, led a successful action against the breaking of an overtime ban by a foreman, contrary to an agreement with the management.

Significantly too, as a consequence of the Coal Board's pit closure programme, a number of miners from closed collieries were directed to the Workshops. This brought an influx of militants and Communist NUM branch officials, including John Pratt, Bob Selkirk and Jim Hynd (better known as the Colonel). The influx of these men and their pit experience strengthened the NUM branch within the factory, which had previously been dominated by the 'moderate' craftsmen union.

In the years that followed, the NUM was to grow in strength from just a handful of men and play a more active role within the factory, raising the level of militancy of the workers there. Unfortunately, however, there was also a rivalry between the NUM which was Communist led and the SCEBTA union which was mainly controlled by Labour 'moderates', that was often divisive and hindered joint action.

Also at this time the Workshops, employed a number of local town councillors, William Anderson, who became the Provost, was a Labour Councillor, as were Bert Brownlee and Jim Purdie. I was elected as a Communist Councillor in 1964 and Joe Paterson was elected as an SNP Councillor for Crosshill, John Wilkie, was elected a Labour Councillor for Kelty. Later Bob Selkirk, Jnr, was also elected to the Cowdenbeath Town Council.

So the Workshops was a highly political place where there was constant argument and debate of opposing Trade Union and political view points, with many leaflets distributed, papers sold and shopfloor meetings creating a political awareness among the workers that was at an unusually high level. As a consequence the miners strikes of 1972 and 1974 found the workshops men united and solid in support of their union. Of course the successful outcomes of the strikes increased the confidence of the workforce, and further strengthened the standing of the Trade Unions within the factory.

However, the election of the Thatcher government in 1979 created a new atmosphere in industrial relations in the country, and throughout British industry, management began to take a new tough line in negotiations with the trade unions. Within the Coal Board as well, sustained by Tory anti-union legislation, all of the worst elements of management emerged to challenge the role of the NUM nationally and at pit level.

The first Board proposals for a fresh programme of colliery closures were announced in February 1981, but with the miners taking strike action and the government having not yet finalised its preparations to tackle the NUM the Board retreated. But this was merely a postponement of the conflict. The Tory Government had learned the lessons of 1972 and 1974 and were merely completing their preparations to take on and defeat the miners union, with the infamous *'Ridley Report'* the blueprint for their strategy.

This Policy Report produced by Nicholas Ridley MP, in 1978 for the Tories set our a strategy for weakening the miners, that section of workers most likely to challenge a future Tory Government seeking to attack wages and impose redundancies. The plan proposed to:-

* Build up coal stocks especially at power stations
* Make contingency plans for the import of coal
* Encourage hauliers to recruit non-union labour
* Introduce dual coal/oil firing in all power stations
* Cut off the money supply to strikers and make the union finance them
* Establish a large mobile squad of police to deal with picketing.

Once elected in 1979 the Tories put this strategy into motion – with great success as it turned out.

A series of events from 1981 to 1983 emboldened the Government and gave them the confidence to renew their attacks on the miners. Significantly in November 1981, the leadership of the NUM failed to win a ballot of their members for industrial action against the wage claim that the Board had offered, although a month later Arthur Scargill became the new President.

The following year the leadership was again unsuccessful in getting the men to vote for a recommendation to take industrial action over the 1982 wage offer, even though the wages issue was linked in the ballot with the question of colliery closures. Encouraged by these ballot reversals the Board began their colliery closure programme.

In Scotland this meant the end for Kinneil Colliery and then later Cardowan Colliery and despite the efforts of the Scottish Union leaders they could not get the response from the work force in the industry for industrial action.

The re-election of the Thatcher Government in June 1983, followed by the appointment of Ian MacGregor, a 71 year old American, in September, fresh from his decimation of the Steel Industry heralded a fresh attack on the miners. MacGregor made it clear he intended to do to the coal industry what he had accomplished at British Steel. His appointment was seen as a direct challenge to the NUM and everyone in the industry, from top management to the pit workers sensed that a confrontation was bound to come sooner or later. Few could have envisaged how serious that confrontation would be.

In the coalfields there was still reluctance to take action against the closure programme, and even when the miners at Monktonhall Colliery went on strike for several weeks, they had to go back at the end without having gained the full support of the rest of the Scottish miners.

A major deterrent to strike action was that as part of the Government strategy for reducing the industry, they had introduced, new, better redundancy terms for miners, and in many pits this affected the attitude of older men, who saw the opportunity to leave the industry after years of hard work, with sums of money they could never hope to save, as well as a reasonable weekly income. The attraction of redundancy was undoubtedly an undermining factor among miners, and weakened the overall unity at the collieries threatened by closure.

As in the rest of the Scottish coalfield, the union delegates at Cowdenbeath Workshops, Jim Hynd (NUM) and Tom Galloway(SCEBTA) did their best throughout to win their men to take action, but were in the main unsuccessful. Of course the attraction of redundancy terms being offered also influenced a number of the older men to leave the Workshops. Unfortunately, this included several union officials, and partly by the attraction of the terms but also with the frustration of failing to get action against pit closures, both unions lost their leading figures.

I'm sure that later during the Strike, some of them regretted their leaving at so crucial a time, but never-the-less the effect was that when the 1984 Miners Strike, broke out in March, the most experienced members of the unions, who had led the 1972 and 1974 Strikes were no longer within the Workshops.

Leadership of the NUM was in the hands of new young Communist officials, Brian Russell (24) and Bryan Easton (22). The SCEBTA Delegate was by now John Simpson, an experienced former Labour Councillor but some of the traditional 'moderates' had now gone to be replaced by younger and more militant committee members. None of those mentioned had been involved in the leadership of the previous national strikes in 1972 and 1974.

The exceptions to this pattern of inexperience were Eddie Garvie, a foreman and COSA (Colliery Staff) representative, and Jack Allan, the NUM Branch Treasurer, both Communists, who were to be tested to the utmost the 12 months ahead, and played an outstanding stabilising role in the Cowdenbeath Strike Centre.

CHAPTER 4

IN THE BEGINNING

Whilst a number of strikes by miners, in the Welsh and Scottish Coalfield had not been able to attract national support, the announcement by the Coal Board, of the closure of Corton Wood and Bull Cliff Collieries in the powerful Yorkshire Area, was the spark which set off the national action. The Board had given notice that they had intended to remove four million tons of capacity from the industry with the consequent loss of 20 pits and 20,000 jobs in the coalfields during the following 12 months. But with the actual announcement of the intended closure of Corton Wood, the Yorkshire Area Executive on the 9th March, declared an area strike and called on others areas of the Union to support them. Meeting on Wednesday the 7th March, the Scottish Area Conference answered that call by deciding that the Strike would start in Scotland on the following Monday.

The decision of the Scottish Executive was met with mixed reactions within the Workshops. Everyone recognised that the Board was determined to carry out massive colliery closures, and that indeed the clash was inevitable. MacGregor, backed by the Government had thrown down the gauntlet and the miners had no alternative but to pick it up. Later, critics would argue that the miners had chosen the wrong time, to go on strike, but the reality was that the miners did not pick the time nor choose the ground. The Government had long prepared their plans in line with the Ridley Report and the Board selected the actual moment to announce the closures, knowing they were virtually certain to get the response that took place.

As in other places there were a variety of opinions among the Workshop men. For some the strike had been too long in coming, but others were reluctant. Indeed at a pre-strike meeting in Lochore, of the West Fife Branch of COSA, Eddie Garvie the Area Rep. failed even to get a seconder to a motion to support a strike. Some felt the call would not be followed by all of the men. Others looking at their personal financial commitments could not see how they could possibly manage through a prolonged dispute. But by far the majority knew it was now or never - the inevitable had arrived.

Over the weekend, there were numerous rumours that Workshops men would not back the Strike, and in particular union officials were concerned about the transport drivers, who had in the past been regarded as the most compliant section of the workforce. However, early on the Monday morning, when Jack Allan and Frank Kirby the union officials went to the Workshops to picket the gates, they found that out of the entire workforce only two foremen - Cummings of the Electric shop and Young of the Cable shop went through the picket line. Actually neither of these two men lived in Cowdenbeath itself. However, for their strike breaking they were dubbed as 'Super Scabs' and when the Strike was ended both 'took their redundancy money and ran' as quickly as possible.

As in the 1974 Strike, it was decided that the Strike Centre, would be in the Miners Institute, and on Monday morning the members of the committees, of the NUM, SCEBTA and COSA along with some miners who lived in Cowdenbeath but worked in the surrounding collieries, held their first meeting.

Cowdenbeath was indeed the first Strike Centre in Fife to be established and at that meeting the Strike Committee elected their officials as follows:-

Chairman:-	Brian Russell - NUM
Joint Secretaries:-	Bryan Easton - NUM*
	David Miller - SCEBTA
Joint Treasurers:	Jim Hardie - SCEBTA
	Jack Allan - NUM
Press Officer:	George Kent - NUM
Workshops Committee members:-	Eddie Garvie - COSA
	Harry Robertson - NUM
	John Simpson - SCEBTA

Footnote: Note - Bryan Easton was the great-grandson of the famous William Easton, jailed for 12 months in the 1921 'lock-out' as described in Chapter 2.

IN THE BEGINNING

	Frank Kirby – SCEBTA
	Robert Ross – SCEBTA
	Harry Cunningham – SCEBTA
Colliery Representatives:	Gordon Wilson – NUM Solsgirth
	Ian Chalmers – NUM Seafield
	Willie Muir – NUM Frances

The Representatives to the Fife Area Strike Committee Headquarters at Dysart were Iain Chalmers and Harry Cunningham.

It was also decided that Harry Cunningham would act as Picket Organiser, and Gordon Wilson offered to take on the important responsibility of managing the Soup Kitchen in the Strike Headquarters.

The Fife Leadership in the Strike – outside Dysart Headquarters.

The political composition of the Strike Committee was six Communists, four Labour, one SNP and three members with 'left sympathies.'

At the Dysart Strike Headquarter, the key figures were Willie Clarke (NUM) and Peter Fenton (SCEBTA) as Joint Chairmen, George Davie(NUM and John Nicol (SCEBTA) as Joint Secretaries, Sandy

Sneddon (SCEBTA) Administration. John Mitchell (NUM) Picket Co-ordinator and John Neilson (NUM) with a special role of building solidarity links throughout the East and North of Scotland.

This leadership too was dominated by Communists which as explained earlier had been the pattern for many years in Fife. At Scottish level the NUM President Mick McGahey and George Bolton, the vice-President were also Communists and along with Eric Clarke, a left-wing Labour Party member as Secretary were the principal officials in the Scottish Coalfield.

Communist presence therefore was very strong at each level of authority in the Strike organisation - Scottish, Fife and Cowdenbeath - and was to exert the decisive influence on, how the Strike was conducted, how public support for the miners was sustained, and helps explain the failure of the Coal Board to get the return to work they were achieving elsewhere.

In the course of the Strike there were to be some changes in the Cowdenbeath leadership. Tom King (SCEBTA) and Arthur Scott (NUM) came on the Committee after a few weeks. George Kent and David Miller resigned due to ill health, Jim Hardie gave up his Treasurer's post after a disagreement in the Committee, and Willie Muir took on extra responsibilities for picketing, when Harry Cunningham moved home.

It was significant that whilst SCEBTA were by far the biggest union in Cowdenbeath Workshops, the key positions on the Strike Committee were held by the NUM representatives (who were also Communists) and as the Strike progressed they played an increasing leading role. When asked about this later, Eddie Garvie, the most experience and astute member of the Strike Committee, said that he felt that the SCEBTA officials were '*almost relieved*' that others were prepared to take on the huge responsibilities involved in such a strike situation.

However, he believed that the traditional militancy in the NUM, the Scottish Area policy of training it's young members at union schools, and the greater political awareness of the Communists of what was at stake, fitted them better to take the leadership. Certainly the evidence as the Strike progressed, confirmed that assessment, as Cowdenbeath Strike Centre was acknowledged as one of the best organised local Centres in Scotland.

IN THE BEGINNING

With the Strike Committee thus set up, they then considered their priorities. These were identified as combining three aspects of work. Firstly, looking after the physical well-being of the strikers and their families, secondly, the organisation of forces for picketing and demonstrations and thirdly generating the propaganda required to maintain the morale and solidarity of the strikers, and to win the support of the General Public.

With those objectives as their guide the Committee got down to the detailed business of organising the Strike Centre drawing on the experience of the two previous National Strikes. The Miners' Institute would be the hub of all their activities, acting as Soup Kitchen, Advice Centre, and meeting place.

Gordon Wilson who had volunteered to lead the Soup Kitchen work had to move quickly. He enlisted immediately his wife Heather, who had canteen experience and she in turn brought along her two cousins Lorraine Adams and Doreen Meldrum who were sisters in a family where the father was a miner. Both these women were unemployed and they added another unemployed girl Liz Bowman to complete the initial Soup Kitchen Team.

As quickly as possible they begged, borrowed and 'acquired' the tools of the trade and with the first donations of food and money the Soup Kitchen was in being within 48 hours. Gordon was to do a first class job, and the women, who had only begun with the desire to help out in the Kitchen were to develop in the course of the strike as key figures in the Women's Support Group.

Along with the preparations for the Soup Kitchen the Strike Committee made their appeal to the Cowdenbeath Public. In a press statement they outlined the miner's case, drew attention to the high unemployment locally, and the need for a thriving coal industry in Fife, and called on the people of the town to give their traditional support to the miners. They also informed their members of the setting up of the Strike Centre where they could be fed, receive advice on benefits and be involved in the meetings, picketing and demonstrations.

Thus within a few days the organisational structure was completed, the Strike Centre established and the local campaign launched. How long the Strike would last no one knew. Amongst themselves the strikers made their own estimates. The most politically aware recognised they faced a daunting task against a determined and ruthless government.

But no one forecast that they had embarked on the most bitter and desperate conflict in living memory, and that it would last for twelve months. Whatever their misgivings, they accepted that the strike had been inevitable, and now it was under way, they had to get on with it. Later, Lorraine Adams confessed that she thought the strike would only last a couple of weeks!

THE INITIAL RESPONSE

When the Strike Committee issued their appeal for support, there was an immediate response from the community. Although there were now only about 360 people in Cowdenbeath, working in the coal industry nevertheless almost every other family had a past or present connection with mining. Also the miners had always been recognised as the most generous towards any local charitable cause and consequently there was widespread sympathy for the men on strike.

Because the Communist Party had a major representation on the Strike Committee, it was natural that they should be the first local political organisation to respond. Meeting on the evening the Strike broke out, they issued a statement declaring their full support for the miner's cause, pointing out that their struggle was not just an issue for miners alone, but was part of a Government attack on the whole Trade Union Movement. They called for solidarity action by other unions to ensure that no coal was produced or existing stocks moved. They made an initial donation (the first recorded donation from any organisation in the accounts) and urged the people of the town to give the maximum financial support.

This political lead was followed soon after by the local Labour Party, who also pledged their support and a donation, and then later by the Scottish National Party Constituency Committee. The Communist Party also were the first (and only) party to hold a public meeting in the town, supporting the miners cause, when George Bolton (Scottish Vice-President NUM) was the main speaker in the Masonic Hall, a few weeks into the Strike.

But whilst the local Labour Party held no public meetings at all during the Strike, on the other hand the Labour controlled local authorities to their credit reacted quickly to the strike situation, acknowledging the practical difficulties the miners and their families faced. The Regional Council decided on a package or measures, which included interest free loans to counter hardship, free meals for miners children and offered to open up Regional buildings as Heat Centres if this became necessary.

They also agreed to allow the miners to use recreational and community facilities free of charge and urged the Gas and Electricity Boards not to disconnect supplies to striking miners for non-payment of bills. This response from the Regional Council was indicative of their historic connections with the mining industry, and it was with deeply felt emotion that Regional Convener Gough publicly declared that *'there will be nae bairn in Fife with an empty belly as long as I am Convener'*

Dunfermline District Council also announced that they would make the maximum permissible rent and rate allowances to council tenants, and that arrears would not be pressed. In practice this meant that for some families, where there was no wage earner at work, no rents or rates were paid at all for the duration of the Strike.

A few weeks later they were also persuaded to open up their recreational facilities to the miners free of charge at agreed times. This deal was negotiated on behalf of the Strike Committee by John Simpson and Eddie Garvie, at a special meeting with Council Officials and the Labour Provost Bob Mill, with some of his colleagues, who were only too pleased to be able to help the men on strike. The result was the Council facilities such as the Swimming Pool, Sauna and Turkish Baths were free to miners outside peak periods.
The Strike Committees were empowered to issue Authorisation Cards and over the summer period many of the men took advantage of these concessions.

The Strike therefore began with the support of the local political parties (there was no Tory Party or Liberal Party in Cowdenbeath), the Local Authorities other trade unions in the area and virtually the whole of the Community. All of the local shopkeepers were approached by the Strike Committee and overwhelmingly they responded by donations of money and food.

The first public street collection was a novel idea. It was organised by the

Communist Party who placed a decorated miners' barrow in a prominent place on the High Street and invited shoppers to drop in some items from their shopping bags or put money in the collecting cans which were at hand. This was an instant success and within two hours the barrow was filled with £100 worth of groceries and there was around £100 in the collecting cans.

In Cowdenbeath the barrow with the Women's Support Group in attendance became a regular feature on the High Street and was always successful. Indeed the idea was copied in many other places in Britain and was equally well received. Those of us who were involved, found it a moving experience on many occasions as pensioners, youngsters and people who obviously had little themselves handed over their donations of food or cash to help the mining families.

Of course there was a lot of fun too, and I can recall that first day when two old folk put some coins in the collecting can and then helped themselves to some groceries out of the barrow. We didn't have the heart to tell them we weren't selling the goods so they went away happy to get a bargain.

Strangely at the start the only public sour note in the community came from an unexpected quarter - the Minister of the North Church, the Rev P.C. Rae. He was in the habit of writing the Christian *'Thought for the Week'* in the local paper, the Central Fife Times, and the week after the Strike began he devoted his *'Thought'* to the miners.

In the text he condemned the strikers for rebelling and declared them to be virtually servants of Satan, thereby insulting men who were taking action not to defend primarily their own jobs, but the jobs of fellow miners elsewhere and the future of their families and their communities in other parts of Britain. I found this *'Thought for the Week'* particularly offensive and, in spite of the hazards of attacking a 'man of the cloth' publicly, I took the opportunity in the following edition of the *'Times'* to criticise the Rev Rae and remind him where his Christian duty lay in helping the families in need.

However, in complete contrast the Minister of the Cairns Church, who was also the Workshops Padre, the Rev Bjarnsson offered his help immediately to the miners, and opened his church doors for the receipt of food and money, which he delivered regularly to the Strike Centre as long as the strike lasted.

The Catholic Church, St Brides on the other hand gave no organised assistance to the miners throughout the Strike, by way of food or money to help the Strike Centre, although the local priest Father Murray did speak at one of the weekly strike meetings and expressed support. Of the other religious bodies in the town only the Salvation Army gave a donation.

Also disappointingly during the strike none of the recognised voluntary and charitable organisations came forward to help relieve the obvious distress among the strikers families, but this was more than made up for by the thousands of individuals who made personal donations in the streets and on the doorsteps.

Within the Workshops itself, the reactions of the staff were mixed. They were members of unions which were not on strike and therefore continued to attend work. Among the junior management and clerical staff, there was general sympathy with the objectives of the strike, but of course most of them, as they had done in the previous national strikes of 1972 and 1974, criticised the timing, ignoring the fact that indeed the miners had not picked the time but had been forced to respond to the Coal Board's closure decisions.

At the start they contributed to the Strike Appeal Fund, but in the main this dried up as the strike progressed. The excuse that was voiced was that they could not be sure that the money was being used for providing foodstuffs for the Strike Centre, but was going to subsidise the picketing which was being carried out.

Among the Senior Management there were violently opposing views. On one extreme was myself, the Production Controller, who totally supported the miners publicly and on the other the Manager Mr Tom Martin, a rabid anti-Trade Unionist who treated the strikers with scorn and contempt, and as time went on he became even more bitter and it was as much as I could do to restrain myself when he sneered at the pickets as *'criminals'* and *'scum'*. He was representative of the new breed of management which emerged in the early Thatcher years in the coal industry with no minds of their own, and willing to carry out instructions without question.

In between were some who sympathised with the strikers and donated to their Funds, but nevertheless in the course of the strike carried out work within the Workshops outwith their own duties and against the interests of the strikers. Indeed as the strike went on Mr Bill Hunter the Works Superintendent became an ever more eager tool of his manager in trying to break the solidarity of the strikers.

With the bitter differences between myself and the manager, it was inevitable that conflict would take place and it did!. I can recall his first reaction to the strike breaking out, when in a discussion among the Management team he forecast that within a week or two the *'moderate majority would tramp over the mindless militant minority'* (the union leaders) *'and flood back to work'*.

I replied that he obviously knew nothing about the men at Cowdenbeath, and that after a few weeks attitudes in fact would harden. Men who may have been reluctant to strike initially change their views and loyalty to their union and to each other becomes paramount. This proved to be the case but I must confess that I, just as much as he, never thought the strike would go on for that long twelve months. I should say that over the year he continued to make the same kind of forecasts which consistently failed to materialise.

CHAPTER 5

CHRONOLOGY OF THE STRIKE

This chronology of the strike is a combination of the important national developments linked to local events, which will not only trace the pattern of the strike, but should also revive personal memories for those who were involved.

MARCH

6th Yorkshire Miners called out over Cortonwood and Bulcliffe wood closure threat. Scottish Miners put on *'Strike Alert'*

9th Durham and Kent Miners and Leaders agree to support Strike. Notts calls for pit-head ballot.

12th The National Strike begins. Only half the 184,000 men on Strike. Flying pickets move into Nottingham and other areas.

In Cowdenbeath (and Fife) strike is virtually solid, despite earlier doubts. The Strike Centre set up, Committee Officials appointed. Soup Kitchen organised and appeal for public support made.

15th David Jones, aged 24, dies during picket in Notts. *'as a result of a heavy blow'* Iain Chalmers and Harry Cunningham represent Cowdenbeath at the Funeral.

19th Notts Miners say they will continue to work.

Local Trade Unions, Councils, Labour, Communist and SNP branches and the townspeople rally round the mining families.

24th First Mass Rally in Dunfermline. Mick McGahey and Gordon Brown MP as main speakers. McGahey call for solidarity action. Fife

Convenor Bert Gough pledges *"there will be nae miner's bairn wi' an empty belly in Fife as long as I am Convener"*.

Miners guarantee supplies of coal to the old, sick, disabled, schools and hospitals.

Power Unions advise members to cross picket lines.

Pickets move into action at Westfield and Nellie Opencast and at Longannet Power Station.

26th NUM leaders tell TUC to keep out of dispute.

31st NOP poll reveals 51% of miners would vote for Strike with only 34% against.

APRIL

3rd NUR railwaymen ordered to boycott coal movement.

5th Notts miners and steelworkers vote to work normally.

Local miners attend STUC Rally in Glasgow.

Soup Kitchen in Miners Welfare now in full swing. One hundred people daily being served. Donations pouring in from other unions, factories, shopkeepers and the townspeople.

Weekly public meetings at Strike Centre begin. George Bolton, Vice-President Scottish NUM warns *"be under no illusions, MacGregor wants only 100,000 miners in 100 super pits, but not here in Scotland"*

11th Pit Deputies Unions (NACODS) votes in favour of Strike action, but not with required two-thirds majority.

12th NUM leaders agree that majority required for Strike should be changed from 55% to simple majority. Neil Kinnock, Labour leader backs a ballot.

14th MORI POLL shows 68% to 26% in favour of Strike.

Miners barrow appears for first time in Cowdenbeath High Street, manned by Communist Party members, to collect money and food.

Fife Regional Council votes 26-15 for package of aid measures for miners.

CHRONOLOGY OF THE STRIKE

Dunfermline District Council follow suit.

Picketing continues at factories, opencast sites and Ravenscraig steelworks.

20th Scargill says Electricity Board had only nine weeks stock of coal.

24th MacGregor refuses to meet Scargill and Scargill refuses to meet MacGregor.

25th NCB launches advertising campaign in press to persuade miners to go back to work.

MAY

3rd British Steel arranges lorry loads of coal to picketed Steelworks.

Cowdenbeath pickets involved in *'ten days of horrific police violence at Hunterston Port and Ravenscraig Steelworks'*

9th In "Day of Action" called by TUC, Fife Miners lead 5000 marchers in Dundee. Workers at Mossmorran and Bus drivers stop work. Fire Brigade only handling emergencies and partial stoppage at Rosyth Dockyard.

12th NUM guarantee coal supplies to threatened Ravenscraig steelworkers.

13th 10,000 women march in rally at Barnsley

14th Scargill claims Electricity Board will be in desperate trouble within a few weeks, and ultimate aim of Strike is downfall of Thatcher Government.

17th Gordon Brown MP condemns tough line taken by DHSS
'the families of miners are being persecuted'

Sponsored walk, Concerts and Football Matches raise money for Strike Centre.

23rd Scargill meets MacGregor for first time since Strike began and declares the 60 minute discussion *'a complete fiasco'*.

25th Convoys of lorries take coke from Orgreave Coking Plant to Scunthorpe Steelworks.

29th The 'Battle of Orgreave' begins - Police use riot gear for first time. Scargill arrested and charged with *'obstruction'*

30th 400 women attend Rally in Lochgelly Centre *'The atmosphere was electric'*.

JUNE

1st Kinnock condemns violence *'on both sides'*

3rd Children's Picnic to Aberdour cancelled due to rain - transferred to Broad Street Community Centre.

5th Daily Mirror reveals Government bought off Railwaymen's pay claim to minimise support for miners.

'Battle of Cartmore' begins. No violence at Nellie Opencast Site Lochgelly, but 134 pickets arrested in two days. Gordon Brown MP challenges police tactics.

7th 110 Miners arrested in angry demo at House of Commons involving 45,000 people.

8th NCB and NUM meeting in Edinburgh. MacGregor says *'a degree of realism is entering the discussions'*.

9th *'Here we go, here we go'* ringing in Streets of Edinburgh as 100,000

NUM Gala Day in Edinburgh

take part in Miners Gala Day Parade.

11th Lochgelly Centre packed for Communist Party Rally in support of Miners. McGahey says *'There may be secret meetings but there will be no secret deals'*

The Lord Provost of Aberdeen gives Civic Reception to 10 miners wives during fundraising tour.

13th NUM and NCB meet but after 90 minutes, talks fail. Scargill predicts Strike will last till winter.

15th Joe Green, aged 55, knocked down and killed on Ferrybridge Power Station Picket line.

Cabaret Star 'Christian' headlines a concert in Cowdenbeath Miners Welfare organised by Women's Support Group.

18th 3000 police confront 6000 miners in final round of 'Battle of Orgreave'. Police violence on scale never witnessed in Britain before, using riot shields, batons, horses and dogs to hound down miners.

21st MacGregor warns Strike could drag into 1985 and in letter to NUM members tells them they will never win.

27th Steelworkers leaders say they will take coal from anywhere to keep plants going. Railworkers in London stage 24 hour Strike.

JULY

5/6th Secret talks resume - At first *'hopeful'*

9th Talks continue and both sides talk of *'movement'*

National Dock Strike called over use of 'scab' labour to move coal at Immingham.

18th Talks finally end in stalemate with NCB insisting on closure of pits *"which couldn't be beneficially developed"*.

21st Major blow to miners as Dock Strike is called off.

300 miners and families enjoy Open Air rally at Lochore Meadows Country Park. Alec Falconer and Mrs Betty Heathfield are the main speakers, Mrs Heathfield declares *"I am proud of what women are doing*

in this dispute. We are backing our men all the way".

Numbers at Strike Centre increase sharply as hardship bites. Fife Regional Council set up Miners Relief Fund.

Willie Hamilton MP attacks miners strike in parliament and calls for national ballot.

24th **Development of working miners groups - led by 'Silver Birch' (Chris Butcher)**

28th NUM and TUC hold tentative talks.

30th South Wales NUM fined £50000 for contempt for ignoring injunction to ban secondary picketing.

31st Chancellor Nigel Lawson says strike has cost £300-350 million so far but it is *"a worthwhile investment for the good of the nation"*.

AUGUST

7th Two Yorkshire miners Ken Foulstone and Bob Taylor, backed by Tory funds, plan to take NUM to court for failure to take a ballot.

9th Cowdenbeath Strike Centre features in 'Newsnight' report on Strike. Cameras also at North End Park to film Jim Leishman, Dunfermline Athletic's Manager score a *'Cracking goal'* in miners Charity Match.

Two faces at Castlehill Pit closed, bringing total closures to twelve during Strike.

11th 25,000 women attend a massive rally in London, delivering black flowers to Mrs Thatcher and a petition to the Queen. Eight Cowdenbeath women are there and say *'It was brilliant!'*

18th Scargill says *'The nearer we get to our biggest ally General Winter, the weaker our opponents position will be'*

3000 March in rain at Miners demonstration in Cowdenbeath to a mass meeting at Cowdenbeath FC Football park. Speakers include McGahey, Gordon Brown, Peter Heathfield, Alec Falconer and Denis Skinner.

At the same time other members of Women's Group hold indoor fete at

YMCA Hall.

20th Alex Maxwell suspended by NCB for *'actions incompatiable with his position in Management'* - for publicly supporting the miners, producing public outcry at *'attack on civil liberties'*.

22nd TUC General Council holds first full scale debate on Strike since it started 5 months ago.

23rd TGWU calls out dockers on Strike again against unloading of 'black coal' but little response to call.

28th Miners and families join in rally at Glenrothes against cuts in the Heath Service.

Fife Regional Council allocates another £122,000 to Miners relief on top of £250,000 already spent or loaned.

30th Polkemet Colliery left to flood. Cowdenbeath men released from Strike duty to help save pit.

SEPTEMBER

3rd TUC votes 10-1 to give more money to miners and for action in support *'wherever this is necessary'*. Resolution opposed by key Unions of Electricity and Power workers, (and never materialised in any significant way).

5 - 9th Talks start again in whistlestop tour beginning in Edinburgh where MacGregor appears with head in plastic bag.

12th NACODS leaders agree to hold ballot and urge Strike action.

14th NUM/NCB Talks break down again.

18th Second Dock Strike called off.

21st Bishop of Durham describes Macgregor as *'elderly imported American'* and calls for his resignation.

Father Murray the local priest of St. Brides Church, just back from Nicaragua, state *'The Miners Strike is an extension of the struggle between the haves and the havenots in this world'*.

Massive fines of from £300 to £750 now being imposed on pickets for the minor offence of 'Breach of Peace'

28th NACODS votes by 82.5% to Strike.

Polls shows miners still support Strike by two to one.

OCTOBER

1st NCB-NACODS talks to avoid Strike.

2nd Kinnock at Labour Party Conference again states that he "*condemns violence by both pickets and police*".

Scargill electrifies the Conference with a magnificent speech -'*probably his finest hour*'. (but promises of essential support again did not materialise)

6 - 8th Series of talks with NCB, NACODS, NUM and ACAS all involved.

NCB tighten up on supply of coal to old, sick and families with babies. Local doctors refuse to issue medical certificates to all '*under five*' children. Women demonstrate in Cowdenbeath Health Centre.

9th George Bolton NUM Scottish Vice President speaks at C.P. meeting in Masonic Hall. "*They have tried to starve us back, they have used bribery and intimidation they have cut off Social Security, they have used the police and the courts to break us -but they will not succeed.*"

11 - 13th Another round of talks between NCB, NUM and NACODS arranged by ACAS.

Womens Group organises fundraising event for wheelchair for disabled woman. '*We still have time to help a deserving cause*'

11th Cowdenbeath Community Council and Miners Unions condemn District Council for installing Gas Heating at new Swimming Pool. "*it makes a mockery of Council's pledge of support for Miners*"

12th Rev. Hugh Ormiston, Industrial Chaplain, speaking in Strike Centre, says "*the Strike is essentially about the right of communities to survive*".

Rev. Bjarnason of Cairns Church compares attack on Coal Mining Communities to '*Highland Clearances*'

15th Pat Lowry ACAS Chief announces failure of talks.

16th NACODS announces first-ever national Strike to start on 25th October.

19th Electricians in Power Stations vote 84% against Strike action.

20th MacGregor replaced by Michael Eaton as chief NCB spokesman

22nd ACAS holds NCB-NACODS talks.

23rd NACODS call off National Strike

25th Judge orders seizure of NUM funds after failure to pay fine.

Jack Allan, Strike Centre Treasurer protects local funds by hiding £4000 *'under the bed'*.

Coal Board steps up newspaper adverts and offers the "Best redundancy terms in Europe".

Local pickets being sent increasingly to Lothians and Ayrshire as drift back to work increases.

Miners Leaders protest at *'excessive force'* being used by Police snatch squads from Lothians.

26th Cowdenbeath Doctors appeal to Coal Board to release coal for all families with children under 5 years of age as *'we are concerned about potential illnesses which may occur'*

31st Talks at ACAS finally collapse.

NOVEMBER

2nd NCB offers Christmas bonus and holiday pay if men go back by 19th

Cowdenbeath miner's 82 year old mother denied concessionary coal despite serious heart complaint.

5th First large return to work takes place. £2 million of NUM funds frozen in a Dublin Bank.

700 miners now back in Scotland but only 50 in Fife.

13th Norman Willis TUC Secretary confronted by hanging noose at

Rally in South Wales.

First serious break in Strike at Cowdenbeath Workshops as 13 men go back in 'armoured' buses. More pickets now needed at Workshops in addition to duties at Ayrshire and Lothians stretching resources to the limit.

16th Arrangements under way for childrens Christmas parties. Community Council donates £200 to help meet costs.

27th Oil Millionaire Paul Getty gives £100,000 to miners hardship fund.

30th Receiver appointed by High Court to handle NUM Funds.

Taxi driver carrying *'working miner'* killed when concrete thrown from bridge lands on Taxi. Three miners charged with murder.

DECEMBER

4th TUC Team meets NUM

9th TUC presses Government and NCB to re-open talks.

14th TUC meets Peter Walker, Energy Minister but no progress.

Return at Cowdenbeath Workshops halts as Christmas draws near.

Town Collection gets *'magnificent response'* Toys and gifts flow in from France, Russia and Belgium as well as other Trades Unions, particularly SOGAT.

Billy Connelly appears in Concert at Lochgelly Centre to raise funds for miners.

17th - 19th & 20th Three Christmas Parties for 250 children held in Cairns Church Hall.

Mining equipment now being shipped out by 'scabs' at Cowdenbeath Workshops for repair by private companies. Scabs accused of *'sabotaging Workshops future when Strike is over'*.

JANUARY 1985

3rd Neil Kinnock joins picket line for the very first time since Strike began.

CHRONOLOGY OF THE STRIKE

5th Scargill tells working miners *'come back out on Strike and we will forgive and forget'.*

Return to work picks up again after Christmas break, but still few at Workshops.

17th Rail Unions stage another 24 hour Strike - against British Rail harassment of railmen blacking coal.

21st 'Talks about talks' take place between NUM and NCB leading to some optimism.

400 men demonstrate at Workshops protesting at threatened closure.

Coal Board propaganda adverts now being matched by full-page replies from Fife Strike Centre. *'It's time for a negotiated settlement'* is the theme.

24th Government stamps on hopes of compromise.

30 Hopes for pit talks dashed. Sequestrators recover almost £5 million of NUM money. (but not the £4000 under Jack Allan's bed!).

25th Local Mining families attend massive STUC Rally in Glasgow. McGahey calls for a *'principled negotiated settlement'.*

FEBRUARY

1st First calls for 'return to work without a settlement' emerge as NCB and NUM seem even further apart.

 2nd Fife's Chief Constable complains of lack of police and wants 150 more. Labour Leader of Council replies *'there seems to be no shortage on picketlines'.*

4th Over 2000 miners return to work nationally.

Frances Colliery closes after fire.

NUM go to ACAS to try and get talks restarted.

7th NCB rules out by talks despite appeal from NUM and NACODS.

11th Bert Wheeler, NCB Scottish Director says *'future of Cowdenbeath Workshops is secure'* Number of returners goes over forty.

12-15th TUC shuttles between NCB and NUM to try and get settlement. Peter Heathfield says two sides *'on eve of breakthrough'*, but shuttle diplomacy breaks down.

19th-21st Another TUC attempt at settlement gets icy response.

22nd Big NCB push to try and get 50% of miners back to work.

24th Mass Rally in London to support miners results in disturbance and 101 arrests in Whitehall.

25th Almost 4000 miners abandon Strike. South Wales and Durham NUM areas call for *'re-appraisal of Strike'*

Local pickets fully stretched trying to cover Fife, Lothians and Ayrshire.

27th NCB claims over 50% of men back at work, but still only 47 at Cowdenbeath Workshops - 85% still on Strike.

MARCH

3rd Special NUM Conference meets and votes narrowly to end Strike.

4th Local Strikers meets in Strike Centre and vote to return to work the next day.

Tues 5th March. It's over! 300 workers march in dignity through Workshops gates, applauded by tearful women.

Strike Committee praises *'magnificent support from the whole community'*.

MP's call for amnesty and Central Fife Times appeals for *'common sense to prevail'* as the campaign for reinstatement of sacked miners begins. But MacGregor promises only that *'miners will pay the price of insurrection'*.

CHAPTER 6

RUNNING THE STRIKE AND STRUGGLING TO SURVIVE

In the 1972 National Strike the Cowdenbeath Labour Club ('The Ritz') had been used as the Strike Centre. In 1974, responding to directions from the NUM nationally to use Miners Institutes wherever they existed, the Cowdenbeath Miners Welfare building in Broad Street was the Strike Centre. For the 1984 Strike once again it became the hub of all the local organisation involved in conducting the Strike.

The Lounge of the Club held around 200 people, and this was the area used to feed the growing numbers who attended the 'Soup Kitchen' daily, and to conduct the weekly meetings on a Friday which the Committee had decided to hold as an essential part of their activities, not only to keep the strikers informed of developments in the Strike but to boost morale with statements of support and solidarity.

In all some forty meetings were held, addressed by the widest possible variety of sympathetic speakers - MP's, Church leaders, Social workers, representatives from other Unions as well as the miners leaders themselves. This was a very important feature of the work of the Cowdenbeath Strike Committee, which was recognised as one of the most effective in Scotland, and certainly was very self-sufficient.

The Committee itself met upstairs in a small room, next door to the primitively equipped kitchen, where the catering group prepared the food, before carrying it downstairs to the Lounge area to be served. Equipment was borrowed from every possible source, including the tea urns which were 'acquired' from Cowdenbeath Workshops itself.

Committee meetings were held every morning, to discuss all the matters related to their responsibilities in the Strike. These included the funding and running of the Soup Kitchen, the arrangements for miners demonstrations and meetings, responding to Coal Board requests for men to deal with emergency work at the collieries and the necessary liaison with the Fife Area Strike Headquarters in Dysart.

All kinds of problems were discussed by the Committee, including sometimes individual cases of hardship, for which special grants would be made. For example assistance with busfare for hospital visits, or indeed a grant for clothing for a child going into hospital. Whilst the latter caused little dissent in the Committee, there were indeed meetings which were not harmonious, as there were often disagreements about what strategy should be followed, or policy adopted in particular circumstances.

For example the specific role that women should play in the Strike was a matter of controversy. Indeed in some other Strike Centres, women were almost barred from becoming involved. In the initial stages only the miners, and not their families, were served in some Soup Kitchens and some Fife womens' groups were totally shunned by their local Strike Committees.

At Cowdenbeath the situation was much better, although a minority group of the Strike Committee unsuccessfully tried to limit their involvement at the start, and continued to resist throughout the Strike. This caused conflict on the Committee, as did other matters like the payment of pickets, and the continual requests from the Workshops management to release men to carry out maintenance work for the pits.

These requests were treated with great suspicion as management repeatedly asked for more men than the Committee considered necessary for the job at hand. The minutes of these meetings frequently record the refusal or scaling down of the manpower requests from the Works Superintendent with the words **'The usual requests for manpower from Hunter were refused'**. They were right to be suspicious because the Workshops management deliberately asked for more men that they actually needed, and were not above having a quiet word with them about coming back to work permanently, when they were on the premises.

The transport of 'Concessionary Coal' and coal for hospitals and schools was another thorny problem. Requests for drivers to deliver this coal and for mechanics to service the vehicles, coming from Peter McCann, the Transport Supervisor were also treated with suspicion.

Similarly the Committee had to deal with reports of coal being illegitimately transported by contractors like Collier's of Crossgates, using NCB drivers who were on strike. Such reports were investigated rigorously until the Committee was satisfied. On one occasion the local coal merchant Billy Reid was also alleged to be dealing in 'scab' coal but was given a public apology when this was found to be untrue.

Those who were authorised to go to work were expected to pay a levy to the Strike Fund, and sometimes this was difficult to extract from the people concerned, with some men just refusing point-blank, whilst others only handed over £1 per shift, and not the £2, which was the levy set.

The variety of problems which arose at the Committee, frequently involved contentious issues, and there were recurring differences of opinion. At times the disagreements could become bitter, and there were one or two resignations from positions during the Strike. However, this was to be expected. When people are in each other pockets for twelve months in such a stressful situation, there are bound to be personal differences and tensions. Indeed the remarkable fact is that although at times angry words were exchanged, in the main broad unity was maintained, and the Committee remained intact and effective to the end.

Charlotte Lindsay serving the Soup

A typical day would begin in the Strike Centre with the women coming in to prepare the food for the day. Throughout the morning, whilst the Committee met upstairs, the striking men and families would congregate and at mid-day the food would be brought downstairs, and served to the waiting queue from tables in the Welfare Lounge. After that it was washing-up time and everybody was expected to pitch in and help. A number of the women would have young children with them and they would be sleeping in their prams or playing about the dance floor. Once the day's chores were done the kitchen staff would sit and relax, some have a smoke whilst they chatted, about their families or the latest happenings in the Strike.

At the beginning of the Strike meals were served to about fifty people, but as the weeks wore on, some 200 families were being fed by the hard core of eight women who manned the kitchen. Whilst at first the food was fairly basic soup, 'mince and tatties' for example, later as confidence grew the cooks became more ambitious and the diet more varied as they tried out some new exotic dish to tempt the palate, with mixed results and sometimes protests. Nevertheless for most of those who dined it was their only square meal of the day and was gratefully received.

Gordon Wilson was in charge of operations in the Soup Kitchen at the start, and he and his team controlled the acquiring of the provisions which were either gifted or in the main bought at the local Cash and Carry, with the money coming in from donations and fund-raising events. The town's shopkeepers were also helpful with perhaps Jimmy Noble one of the local butchers being particularly generous with a weekly provision of meat deserving special mention. Later on Helen Thomson replaced Gordon, as head of the catering staff and a 'workaholic' herself she and the other women did a superb job in difficult circumstances.

All of this of course was not always smooth-going and there were rows between the women and the Strike Committee and indeed among the women themselves. On one such occasion things reached such a pitch of confrontation that at a Strike Committee meeting, Eddie Garvie threatened to sack the women and 'bring in a new team of caterers'. This was a risky line to take, as it was an empty threat, but his bluff wasn't called and 'normal service was resumed'.

After their early morning meeting, the Committee came downstairs, and were available to answer queries and give advice to the strikers, on matters like Social Security Benefits, Rents and Rates Rebates, how to stave off debt collectors, demands from Electricity and Gas Boards, how to deal with Building Societies, Concessionary Coal problems, and a host of other anxieties and queries which worried the families. Harry Robertson, whose wife worked in the Social Security Office in Cowdenbeath became an expert on these matters.

On the notice board there was information about events which were being organised, sheets for taking the names of volunteers for picketing duties or for travelling to rallies and demonstrations, or other information useful to the strikers. The Picket Organiser, at first Harry Cunningham and then Willie Muir, buzzed around tying up arrangements, whilst Jack Allan, the Treasurer received and paid out money with meticulous care, to ensure without question that the books balanced at the end of the day.

During the morning those not on picket duty would sit around discussing the latest developments in the Strike, relating stories of incidents on the picket line or arguing about things they had seen on the TV news and speculating about what might happen next. Others would of course debate the usual topics of football, horse-racing and so on, whilst others would go away and take advantage of the free recreational facilities provided by the Councils to those on strike, with the vouchers provided by the Secretary of the Strike Committee.

Coming together in the Strike Centre on a daily basis they drew strength from each other to combat the lack of money, the frustration and the depression which could have overcome their resolve if they retreated into isolation. For a year they learned to exist on very little. In the case of married men, sometimes wives had part-time jobs which brought in some money. Where this was not the case, the families were entitled to meagre Social Security benefits, but the Government deducted £15 from that allowance on the grounds of 'assumed Strike Pay' which clearly the NUM couldn't pay and was but another Government piece of coercion to try and break the Strike.

Otherwise they were helped by their relatives and friends, as were the young single men, who had no income at all, picking up a pound or two from picket duty, or casual work in the farmers fields picking 'berries' tatties' or turnips. On a few occasions the single men got payments from the 'Relief Fund', and there were also payments from the Regional Council for the children of those on Strike.

The local Welfare Rights Office was heavily involved in helping as well.

Tom Murdoch, the Officer in charge of the office contacted as many Strike Centres as possible at the beginning of the Strike, outlining the limited benefits that were available. Discussions were held with the local authorities to ensure that mining families were sympathetically treated on matters of rent/rates rebates. The Fife Regional Council Social Work Department was pressed to make sure that they carried out their statutory duties in providing assistance to families experiencing hardship. Discussions also took place with the Gas and Electricity Boards to avoid pressure being put on consumers to pay unreasonable amounts towards accounts.

Many cases were handled which involved negotiating with private companies and finance houses to persuade them to be patient assuring them that people from mining communities would honour all their obligations when the Strike ended. This service, of course continued well after the Strike as those involved struggled to recover from the ordeal.

During the strike, under Government pressure, the DHSS decided that payments from the Social Works Department to relieve hardship would be deducted from benefit. The Welfare Rights Office immediately lodged a number of appeals. The cases finally went to the Commissioner and despite the strenuous efforts of the DHSS to deny the claims, the Commissioner ultimately ruled that they had acted unlawfully in making these deductions.

THE MINI-MINERS

With the number of young men involved in the Strike, it was to be expected in a year there would be a number of new 'arrivals'. Indeed on the day the Strike started Janice Russell, the wife of the Strike Committee Chairman gave birth to her son, Jay, ensuring that she at least will never forget that date. The worst of the poverty relieved by her £25.95p maternity benefit and help from parents, nevertheless the family were hard-pushed to cope with the extra expense of a new baby.

This was a real problem for the parents and was recognised by the Fife Strike Committee who examined ways to assist the pregnant women. The City of Dundee responded to an appeal in the finest tradition of solidarity between that city and the miners of Fife. The Dundee Relief Committee took a decision to supply a layette for every pregnant mother in the Fife area. In all they donated over 75 'kits', with workplaces in Dundee each sponsoring a child by providing the layette, chipping in personal gifts, money, knitted mittens, or shawls and so on.

The Mini-Minors in Concert

Apart from Jay Russell, three other babies were born to Cowdenbeath families - Gordon Cunningham, Cameron Ross, and Joan Kirby, and spent a fair part of their first year in the Strike Centre and occasionally on rallies and demonstrations, along with the older children who matured during the Strike, and became regulars at every event, marching, waving their banners and singing their songs. The poems and songs they learnt at their parents sides were not the traditional nursery rhymes; for them the ogres were Thatcher and McGregor, the heroes McGahey and Scargill.

Through the towns and cities of Scotland they paraded for a year, knowing their parents had few treats to give them but revelling in the experience as their young voices rang through the streets chanting '*If you hate Maggie Thatcher, clap your hands*' or '*I'd rather be a picket than a scab*'. They may have not totally understood all that was involved but I have no doubt they learned more about the realities of power in our country and the unfairness of it all during that twelve months than all their modern studies at school could ever teach them.

In all some 267 children were affected by the Strike - 179 below the age of 11, and recognising the particular difficulties these families faced as the strike dragged on several hardship payments were made by the Strike Committee from money donated by the local Authorities, and various support groups, to help alleviate their particular situation.

SOLIDARITY IN ACTION

Whilst everybody in Britain did not agree with the miners struggle, and the slanted presentation of mass picketing and violence they saw on television influenced their views, nevertheless there was in general widespread sympathy for the miners families. In the course of the Strike huge sums of money and other forms of assistance were donated from the general public.

All over Britain relief groups were formed, and miners and their women support groups travelled everywhere collecting money, food and clothing for the cause. Prominent people from every walk of life, not just politicians and union leaders, but sportsmen, actors, musicians, comedians all donated or gave their services free for charity concerts.

Just to mention a few among the long list of celebrities were Larry Adler, Brian Clough, Jack Charlton, Judi Dench, Glenda Jackson, Ben Kingsley, Spike Milligan, Pat Phoenix, Susannah York, Bands UB40 and the Flying Pickets. In Scotland, leading artists like Andy Cameron, Bill McCue, John Cairney, Anne Lorne Gillies, Jimmy Logan, Carol Kidd, Dick Gaughan, and Elaine C. Smith were among the many who rallied to the miners cause.

Locally numerous 'Charity Concerts" were held to raise funds, and Billy Connelly, despite his upwards path to become a friend of the Royals, showed that he had not forgotten his days as a Clydeside shipbuilder, or his early days as a performer in Kelty Working Men's Club ('the Humblebums') and came to Lochgelly Centre Theatre to appear in a show for the miners.

Wildcat Theatre were another group of artists who made a unique contribution to the miners campaign. They toured Scotland with a specially written musical 'Dead Liberty' not only 'spreading the message' but raising money for the Relief Fund. They also presented free shows to the miners and their families, and I recall being at Bowhill Miners Institute along with hundreds of parents and children, many of whom had never attended a musical before, bringing the house down with cheers at the emotional end to a great performance.

The miners themselves had a great reputation of generosity to numerous charitable causes, and never failed to respond to worthy appeals from others. This was recognised by many folk who may not have agreed with the Strike, but acknowledged that the miners had never ignored others in need in the past, and wanted to help them now.

John Neilson, the delegate at Seafield Pit, leading a group of others, had a special responsibility for identifying and securing financial help outside the Fife area and he travelled extensively throughout Tayside and Grampian Regions making contact with local Trade Union organisations and individuals.

Iain Chalmers, who was a delegate from Cowdenbeath to the Dysart Headquarters was another who toured the country building the solidarity campaign, along with Harry Cunningham, establishing links with the Labour Movement in the North East of Scotland, but also visiting the English coalfield areas, and making contacts with the miners there. Iain was away from Cowdenbeath Strike Centre so often that Willie Muir, the Picket Organiser, dubbed him as 'The Foreign Secretary' and the name stuck. However he made a valuable contribution in the solidarity field.

Those who did this kind of work found support for the miners wherever they journeyed and John Neilson would often recount tales of incidents, in Aberdeen, Inverness, Peterhead, Banff, Buckie, speaking to every kind of worker from fishermen to postal workers, from dockers to nurses, raising funds for the mining families.

His particular favourite story was of a mass meeting of Kestrel Marine workers in the Caird Hall in Dundee. There were to be 1000 workers present and before the meeting the Chairman told John he intended to propose a compulsory donation of £5 per head. John was a bit apprehensive at this, but following the debate in the hall about the Strike, the Chairman proposed the levy. After a murmur in the audience John thought his worst fears were to be realised when an elderly figure rose in the audience to challenge the proposal.

Slowly, amidst silence the man walked to the microphone, whilst John felt his heart fall. "Mr Chairman, I want to oppose this proposal for a £5 levy. I can remember being on Strike many years ago, when we were really up against it financially, answering a knock on our office door. I found a man standing there on the doorstep who thrust £100 in my hand, saying I'm John McArthur a Fife Miners Leader and that's from the Miners Union to help you'.
'Mr Chairman, I have never forgotten that and neither should all of us here. Therefore I oppose the £5 levy and I propose £10 instead'. The decision was carried unanimously and the Miners Strike fund increased by £10,000 that day. an example of the feeling that existed in Dundee for the miners.

Outside the Strike Centre – Bryan Easton (Sec.), Jack Allan (Treas.) and Harry Robertson

In Fife almost £300,000 was raised through the Dysart Central Strike Centre, money which was used to run the Centre, hire buses for pickets and demonstrations, conduct meetings, issue publicity and above all help the families to survive. This money was the vital life blood of the strike and of course there was a moment of panic when the National funds were sequestrated, and a rush to get the Fife money out of the Bank.

RUNNING THE STRIKE AND STRUGGLING TO SURVIVE

The local branch didn't have enough cash on hand and three officials from the Strike Centre were dispatched to Edinburgh to withdraw the funds. They made the return journey with £42,000 in notes stuffed in a bag, which then disappeared to a 'safe hiding place' known only to Alex Campbell, the Area Treasurer.

However he proved to be totally trustworthy, didn't 'do a runner' but unearthed the cash again when the coast was clear.

On top of the finance at Scottish and Fife level in the course of the Strike some £18,000 came into the Cowdenbeath Centre's General Fund, £2000 of which was collected in the Street. Donations came from every section of the community, from local factories and businesses, from hospitals and colleges, from individuals who dropped into the Strike Centre with their contribution, and through the post from people home and abroad who wanted to express their solidarity with the mining families. The proceeds from sponsored runs, charity football matches, raffles, 'At Homes' concerts and sales of work all added to the total.

The money was guarded rigorously by Jack Allan the Treasurer, the kind of individual who would not part with a penny that couldn't be justified or accounted for. Every 'phone call had to be legitimate and necessary - every collection counted at least twice, every donation properly recorded, every £2 for picket duty signed for. Money was scarce and had to be used wisely.

Bryan Easton recalls being given £2 for petrol to travel across to Edinburgh. As usual every pint of petrol had to be spun out to the maximum mileage, and Bryan, conscious of the need to economise set off on the road nursing his car every inch of the way. only to grind to a halt on the middle of the Forth Bridge the last drop of petrol gone.

Sitting there, cursing his misfortune to the night air, he saw the breakdown wagon approaching, knowing he faced a penalty for being stuck on the bridge. However, once again the public sympathy for the miners surfaced, and the driver after hearing his tale, towed him to the other side and deposited him in a garage there, where he spent his £2 on petrol, with great relief.

MERRY CHRISTMAS

In addition to the £18,000 raised for the General Fund a special appeal around Christmas brought in £3000, in just five weeks, as the community responded to the unacceptable prospect of children *'that Santa Claus forgot'*. Money came from every quarter. The Community Council handed over £200 and even local businessman Gerard Eadie of 'CR Smith' a notorious anti-union employer who only months before had denied union recognition to his workers, resulting in an unsuccessful strike, felt compelled to donate £100. Money had also come from abroad for the Strike, from French, Belgian and Russian Trade Unions, and from the USA, and at Christmas the French and the Russians sent toys for the miner's children.

The Printing Union SOGAT were especially generous supporters and at Christmas they guaranteed the Christmas dinner, by presenting the miners with thousands of frozen chickens. Cowdenbeath was allocated over 300 birds and the task of delivering them was undertaken in relays by teams including my sons Gordon and Neil. At the time a football team I managed had a minibus, and it was always at the disposal of the Strike Committee, to the great annoyance of Martin the Works Manager. The bus was duly 'loaded to the gunnels' with the frozen chickens and armed with the list of names and addresses the team set off to deliver the Christmas dinners.

Throughout the day they went about their task. being received along the way with great pleasure. In turn each family was supplied, until only a few chickens were left. Making their way down Moss-side Road, on the spur of the moment one of the team requested a stop *'to deliver Billy Williamson's chicken'*. The driver duly obliged and the frozen chicken took flight, propelled by hand through the front window, whilst the minibus sped away.

At the time there was little sympathy for the Williamson family because Billy Williamson was a 'scab' an early strikebreaker, and after nine months on strike hatred and bitterness had overcome Christmas charity. It was not the only occasion his house windows were smashed in the Strike, and his family must have been terrified, but there was no forgiveness in the hearts of those young men who had suffered hardship and deprivation, battled against police brutality at Ravenscraig, Hunterson, Orgreave and elsewhere and been forced to watch helplessly as the armoured buses carrying the 'scabs' through the lines of men, women and children at the Workshops gates each morning.

Despite all the fears and worries about Christmas, the fact is that due to the public response the children were not much deprived. They enjoyed Christmas parties organised by the Women's Group, they got presents donated from various sources, attended Pantomimes in Kirkcaldy and Lochgelly (some for the first time) and had their Christmas dinner provided.

The activity in preparing for Christmas and the Children's parties engaged the minds of many of the Strike Committee, and with the drift back to work arrested over the festive period, questions of how the Strike would end were for the moment put to one side.

The atmosphere in the Strike Centre from the beginning had varied with how he people saw the strike going. A sign of victory raised the spirits, a set back created gloom and as initiative after initiative to settle the Strike had failed, and the months moved on, it became purely a case of holding on. Once the drift back began in earnest around October, the writing was on the wall, and in their heart of hearts they knew only a miracle could save them - and miracles are few and far between.

Once Christmas came and went and the drift back resumed with substantial numbers back in Lothians and Ayrshire, it was difficult to get anyone to discuss what was happening in the Strike. People in the Strike Centre kept themselves busy with their daily chores going through the motions of the ritual they were now used to, trying to avoid facing up to the reality of the defeat which faced them, hanging on grimly because they saw nothing else they could do.

The whole of 1984 had been a test of survival, and they had survived by the massive support of family, and friends, generosity and solidarity from countless numbers of people and organisations, not only in Britain but from every corner of the world. It was a level of assistance over a long period unequalled in British history by any group of workers.

But the unity of all miners in Britain, the industrial action by other workers, and the overwhelming public pressure which may have given them victory was tragically absent. The Government had been ruthless and determined, prepared to use all it's resources to defeat them, and now they smelled blood. The Tories were determined to inflict a savage defeat on the miners and there was to be no honourable settlement.

CHAPTER 7

'A MIRACLE THAT NO ONE WAS KILLED'

These are the words of a Police Commander after the 'Battle of Orgreave' in which according to BBC Television 6000 rioting, violent miners launched a brutal attack on policemen sent there merely to maintain control against picket line violence. Among those 6000 pickets were some forty from the Cowdenbeath Centre who travelled down by bus to what was to be the biggest picket the Strike had seen, a trial of strength between the miners and the police.

Cowdenbeath had right from the start a hard core of pickets, mostly young men, and at first there was a spirit of adventure about it all, soon to be lost as hardship and bitterness grew as the months rolled on. In the first weeks of the Strike the role of the pickets was to try and prevent the movement of coal in the area, as there was virtually nobody trying to go to work at the collieries or the workshops. For example pickets were mounted 24 hours a day to stop trains and lorries transporting coal from the Westfield Opencast site and were successful.

One vivid recollection I have of that time in March was when driving home, in blinding snow from Glenrothes at midnight to be confronted by a lone white ghost like figure on a bridge near Kinglassie, a conscientious young picket doing his duty with enthusiasm. We exchanged greetings as we passed.

The Westfield coal was bound for Longannet Power Station, and here too pickets were mounted to try and prevent coal coming in from other places. As was to be the case elsewhere the police were at hand to prevent the picket being effective. There was much shouting, heaving and shoving but no arrests, although Sean Ferguson from Cowdenbeath was grabbed by the police when in a moment of passion he threw the runt of an apple he had been eating at a passing vehicle. Sean was being led away, but after a word from Eddie Garvie to the arresting sergeant that all he would do was provoke real trouble, Sean was allowed to go free with a word of warning.

Attempts were also made to picket the movement of coal into factories in the area, but after a few abortive efforts at places like Tullis Russell at Leslie, this was abandoned.

The overall strategy at that stage seemed to be to concentrate on stopping the movement of coal to the Power Stations, and the import of coal from abroad. In that regard whilst the dockers at unionised ports were co-operating with the strikers, pickets were dispatched to 'Non-scheme' ports (those not covered by the National Dock Board Scheme and therefore not unionised) to monitor any such ports.

For example Don Taylor hauled his caravan all the way to Inverness to watch for any coal coming into Invergordon, and had two spells of a fortnight there keeping watch, the first with a fellow picket and the second with his wife Sandra. No coal came in to that port in those instances, but the trip was not entirely wasted as Don returned with a cheque for over £1200 from the workers at the Ardesier Construction Yard.

However despite these kinds of activities my own view which I expressed in a special meeting of Communists miners in April chaired by Mick McGahey at the NUM offices in Edinburgh, that indeed there was no clear strategy at all as to how the Strike was to be won, and I'm sure that was the case.

For a period the pickets concentrated on trying to stop coal being shipped in for use at Ravenscraig Steelworks, but there were differences between the miners leaders and the steelworkers who would not countenance the closure of the plant. The pickets were angry and indeed there was little sympathy among many of them when Ravenscraig itself finally was closed in later years.

At the time hundreds of pickets were dispatched to the Hunterston Terminal on the River Clyde, but they were more than matched by the battalion of police who stood guard as the notorious 'Yuill and Dodd' lorries

'A MIRACLE THAT NO ONE WAS KILLED'

thundered through the picket lines. Amongst the Cowdenbeath pickets there was growing feeling that no matter how many pickets the miners sent, they would be more than matched by the growing police ranks. Indeed it was suspected with some evidence, that 'phones were being 'tapped' by the police and additional precautions were taken in communications with Strike Centres and pickets. Not that all picketing was unsuccessful. There was the occasional victory, but only occasional. The most significant one in Fife in the whole of the Strike took place in June 1984, the same month as the dreadful 'Battle of Orgreave'.

'NELLIE' OPEN CAST SITE (CARTMORE INDUSTRIAL ESTATE).

When you consider that whilst there were 83 arrests at Orgreave, there were 134 arrests at 'the Nellie' Opencast Site in Lochgelly, it would seem that the latter must have been the scene of tremendous violence. Nothing could be further from the truth.

The picket at 'the Nellie' began on Wednesday 6th June, when the Strike Centre at Lochgelly got a report of lorries coming to lift coal to take to a Power Station in England. The call went out to the other Strike Centres and soon some 150 pickets arrived including many from Cowdenbeath.

There was the usual heaving and shoving which had become an accepted part of the daily ritual on the picket line, but on this occasion the police

'Heaving and Shoving' – on the Picket Line at Nellie Opencast (Cartmore) Photo: Courtesy of The Dunfermline Press

went over the top. That day they arrested 57 people on the slightest provocation. The following day fresh pickets arrived, again there was the ebb and flow of bodies as the lorries sped out of the entrance, and that day a further 70 pickets had been hauled away to the police cells in Cowdenbeath. There they were held until photographed and finger printed, before being transferred to Dunfermline to be charged.

That second day I had gone to Lochgelly to 'observe' the confrontation due to the number of arrests the day before. I had taken a holiday from work that day and was on the picket line myself - a stupid thing to do because if I had been reported being there, I would surely have been sacked.

However, common sense did not prevail, and I recall staring steadfastly at the row of policeman, before the lorries arrived, noting faces and identity numbers, for some unknown purpose. I stood face to face with Sergeant Tom Ogilvie, a former Stores employee at the Workshops where we played for the same departmental football team. We smiled at each other but I had the feeling that no matter past friendship Tom would have sunk his size 11 boot in me that day just the same. In the event my stupidity dawned on me and I retired to the sidelines, an 'observer' on the scene, monitoring police violence. With 70 pickets arrested it seemed that anyone who moved was a candidate for the police van. A young lad going to collect his wages from one of the factories on the same site was even picked up by the police, led away protesting he had nothing to do with the pickets.

The news flew back to Cowdenbeath Strike Centre as one after another young pickets were arrested. In a sense it became a 'badge of honour' to be 'lifted' by the police - as if you weren't really a fully fledged picket till you had seen the inside of a cell. On the other hand the police had clearly decided to take a tough line to frighten off the pickets and decimate the numbers which the Strike Centres would muster.

That day the lorries again managed to get through, due to the number of police imported from Edinburgh and the Lothians, and I can recall shaking with anger as they sped away in their buses, some of them taunting the miners by waving ten-pound notes at the windows.

But by the third day the scene changed. The lorries had been trailed by

Councillor Joe Paterson from the Lochore Strike Centre to their drop off point in Hamilton and were approaching the Nellie Opencast site from the road through Ballingry. With the route established the people of that mining village reacted and on that third day the lorries were met with great hostility as crowds of local people hurled abuse at the drivers. Pensioners, housewives and children joined in. The final straw for the lorry drivers was when over 100 children instead of going into school, marched out on to the road singing and shouting and blocking the path of the worried lorrydrivers.

The action of the youngsters who marched over a mile down the road, added to the mass picketing at the opencast site seemed too much for the scab drivers, and they never re-appeared. A victory at last for the pickets, but at a price - the arrest of 134 pickets.

THE BATTLE OF ORGREAVE

But if the picketing at the Nellie was a cause for celebration, the authorities more than evened the score at Orgreave. The call had gone out from Scargill and the Union leadership for a mass picket at Orgreave Coking Plant in Yorkshire. From the 29th March there had been serious trouble on the picket lines there, but this was to be a major test of strength, with Scargill looking for the kind of decisive victory achieved in 1972 at the Saltley Coke Works in Birmingham.

The miners came from all over the country. Cowdenbeath Strike Centre had more names than seats on the bus which carried the forty pickets, and they set off in high spirits. The Scottish men had already tasted the brutality of the police at Hunterston and Ravenscraig, the charging horses, the flashing batons and the riots shield, and they thought they had just about seen it all.

As they sped through the night across the English border, they were relishing the day that was to come. This was the big one. After the pounding they took at Hunterston and Ravenscraig they were anxious for a victory on the picket line which would turn the tide of the Strike in their favour. Little did they know that they were heading for the most vicious calculated battering ever witnessed in modern times.

The police set them up, there is no doubt. Whereas on previous occasions pickets would be turned back by road blocks and police vehicles, this time the roads were thrown open and they were waved through - an invitation to slaughter.

There have been many descriptions of the scene but for me the most vivid picture was given to me by Jack Allan, the Strike Centre Treasurer. *"Alex, there we were moving towards the site, the lads in tee-shirts, jeans and trainers, laughing and singing on a beautiful sunny day, being ushered into position by the police. And then there in the distance the sun glistened on the police riot shields. Did you ever see the movie 'Spartacus' with Kirk Douglas. It was just like that. A ragged peasant army moving towards the Roman Centurions, to engage in a battle that could only have one outcome - our massacre".*

The charges at Orgreave were the most brutal that had been seen in Britain this century, even worse than in 1921 and 1926. Time and again the police charged, with riot shields, batons, horses and dogs, and the pickets ran for their lives, those who stopped to help a mate being rewarded by a police truncheon. Despite the distortion of Television and the Press who depicted the pickets as a rioting mob attacking the police, twice as many miners as police were seriously injured and there was no mercy shown to those who fell as they ran away.

The Cowdenbeath lads recall a picket running straight through the glass of a greenhouse to get away, others being pursued through the interior of an ASDA supermarket by mounted policemen, in and out of houses, and over railway lines. They hid under bridges, run or crawled through fields and trees, hotly pursued by the bloodthirsty cavalry. Yet even in the midst of this terror Bryan Easton can recall an incident which made him laugh then and still does. *"there I was 22 year old, running for my life up a hill, when Jackie Allan who was at least twice my age shot past me like a streak of lightning"*.

But it was not a time to be a hero - the police weren't handing out medals, they were intent on inflicting punishment, and it was a case of 'de'il tak the hindmost'. Fortunately none of the Cowdenbeath men were seriously injured or arrested, and one way or another they finally got out of it all, and managed back to their bus. They travelled home, shocked and despaired by an experience they would never forget. And it was sombre bus which finally crossed the River Forth to the safety of their home town.

All this time in the Strike Centre the waiting wives had watched events on the giant television screen, some in tears, and overcome with anxiety for their husbands safety, angry that they had been treated with such great brutality, but desperate to see them return in one piece, even if shattered by their experience.

Orgreave was certainly a significant turning point in the Strike. It was now clear to everyone that the Government would spare no effort to defeat the miners. The whole affair was conducted like a military action, with ruthlessness and ferocity on a scale that none of us ever imagined. It will go down in history as one of the blackest days in British history, but also the event that proved conclusively that mass-picketing would not win the Strike.

ON DUTY AT BRIGHILLS.

Not all the picketing was as dramatic as Orgreave or the Nellie Opencast. In the first half of the Strike the efforts was concentrated in trying to prevent the movement of coal, including the import of coal from abroad. Later the emphasis had to move to picketing at the pits and Workshops as the drift back to work began.

However as part of the plan to stop the movement of coal, a picket was set up at Brighills, which lay at the bottom of the hill on the road from Lochgelly to Bowhill. The responsibility for this was laid on the Cowdenbeath and Lochgelly Strike Centre and every day between 12 noon and 5 pm, two shifts of two pickets taking $2 \, 1/2$ hours each would man the 'howf' at the entry to the site, just on the bend of the road.

The Cowdenbeath Picket Book religiously maintained by Willie Muir shows the names of those who carried on this picket for a year. Harry Robertson, Jack Allan, Neil Maxwell, John Veale, Tam Hoggan, Tom King, Andrew Leishman, Bryan Easton, Davie Rattray, Jimmy Bell, John Lindsay, Gordon Maxwell and so on. All the regular pickets would take a turn and for their task they would get £2 a day subsistence with maybe 10 cigarettes for the smokers.

The media would often talk during the Strike about pickets getting paid as though huge sums were being used from Strike funds which were meant to feed the strikers families. Some 'highly principled' people even questioned the £2 paid to the pickets for their duty at Brighills.

My son Gordon, a front-line picket throughout the Strike, and one of the Brighill Regulars said later *"It always puzzled me why the Union insisted on constant manning at the 'outpost at Brighills' Was it a token gesture or just a reason to give hard-up miners £2 and a packet of fags?"*

If the truth were told the latter was the reason. There was never any attempt to take coal out from that site during the Strike, and the picket wasn't really necessary. But the Strike Committee were able to give a few pounds to men who had virtually nothing in this way, and could justify it on the basis of the 2 1/2 hours picket duty meriting 'Subsistence'.

Brighills is forever carried in the memory of those who mounted that endless picket, and even today as I pass the spot I still look for the two pickets sitting in the 'howf' watching the world go bye.

'UNDERCOVER AGENTS'

As part of their responsibility for picketing the movement of coal Cowdenbeath Strike Centre also helped to man the docks at Perth to intercept foreign coal. Armed with binoculars a couple of strikers would scan the River Tay watching for coal ships arriving. Once spotted the alarm would be sounded and the picket army would assemble to confront the lorries waiting to take the coal away.

Amidst all the serious events of any Strike there are always humourous stories and Gordon (Maxwell) recalls one of these at a particularly violent picket at Perth in June 1984

"We gathered there, about two hundred of us, trying to stop coal being unloaded. Then two lorries were loaded from the ship berthed at the dockside. The dock road was amass with pickets and police, and once the lorries moved out, mayhem broke out.

The lorries retreated back to the ship and order was restored. A tense truce held until the police re-grouped and prepared for another run, The pickets were on the dockside with only ten feet of water between them and the ship. At the stern of the ship the foreign crew had assembled to watch the proceedings, among them were two 'ladies' (a term used loosely in this case) who on seeing the hostile crowd retired to their quarters.

At that moment the lorries 'fired up' and prepared to advance. Some of the pickets surged across the road, but the main body of men remained at the dockside, packed around the berth. The two women had reappeared, singing and dancing in their 'birthday suits' (although these suits looked in need of an iron). The coal lorries thus made their escape as miners cheered, and in fact one fell into the water as he strove to get a closer look. Rumour has it that the Perth Police had used two 'undercover' agents to act as decoys. And indeed it was successful, although on the day dozens of miners were arrested and the Police read the Riot Act before they waded in among the pickets".

Early morning on the Picket line at Seafield, with Alec Falconer MP

That was life on the Picket line, a harsh business, sometimes relieved by a humourous incident often re-told with great joy in later years.

Another such story was the night that a bus load of pickets stood outside the Strike Centre bound for a Power Station in the north of England. Just before it was due to leave there were two late arrivals, Tom Hoggan and Willie Jones, at least one of them 'slightly inebriated'. They were hustled on to the bus and stretched out on a seat apiece they soon fell into a slumber.

The bus roared on down the highway, but eventually responding to the clamour of the passengers to *'stop for a slash'* (relieve the call of nature) the bus drew up. Tom, awakening from his sleep, was one of those who just had to go, and alighting unsteadily from the bus, he looked around in bewilderment. *'Hey are we at Stevensonbeath yet*? (a housing scheme in Cowdenbeath) he enquired to roars of laughter. Perhaps a severe lesson for Tom on the evils of drink, but a hilarious moment for the others and an extra two 'volunteers' on the picket line.

ARRESTING THE DRIFT BACK

By November, nine months into the Strike, the first real drift back to work had begun, and now the task of the pickets moved from trying to stop the movement of coal to picketing the collieries where men were going back.

The Fife pits were still almost solid with less than 50 people having returned, but there were serious problems elsewhere in Scotland particularly at Bilston Glen, in the Lothians. The Fife men were now concentrating in stemming the flow back to work, and were travelling to the Lothians, Ayrshire and Lanarkshire to bolster those still on strike, at the same time mounting substantial pickets at their own collieries and the Workshops.

Over the Christmas period the drift back was arrested, but by January the collieries in other parts of Scotland were getting back into production with the return of the miners there, although Fife had still 95% out. By now also as well as being arrested and charged, pickets were being sacked by the Coal Board. Indeed some men like Ronnie Campbell from the Workshops never worked again in the industry whilst others like Jimmy Whyte were victimised for months after the Strike was ended. This was another pressure on the pickets, and a deterrent to taking part.

My third son Neil, who was a consistent picket throughout the Strike and travelled all over the country was one who just managed to escape the sack. It was at Bilston Glen he was arrested, in August 1984. He had travelled with a bus load of strikers to the Pit and joined the few hundred men already on the Picket line. Confronted with this mass picket the Police Inspector ordered his constables to *'grab some of them'* and they dived in among the crowd and seized at random 10 men, Neil being among them and he was drawn by the hair to the waiting police van.

But even in the grimmest situation the unexpected can happen. Neil recalls when he was arrested and taken to the cells in Edinburgh *"there were about a dozen of us taken in a big blue van and dumped in beside another 20 lads already there, mainly from Steelend* (a mining village in Fife). *The guys were all hardened miners, and by their looks and coughs probably heavy smokers. They were all gasping for a fag as they paced up an down the cell. Suddenly there was a clanking of keys, a small hatch in the door slid open an a ten packet of cigarettes pushed through. A huge sigh of relief resounded throughout the cell as the cigarettes were grabbed and passed round. The identity of the sympathiser was never established, but it just shows how we got support in the strangest of places".*

He spent the night in police cells, was charged the next day with Breach of the Peace and on 18th February was fined £35 on the word of a policemen who 'wouldn't have known him from Adam' but was prepared to identify him as a criminal. For weeks we worried if he would also lose his job, but thankfully no further action was taken.

During January, Neil like all the other regular pickets from Cowdenbeath was picketing not just at Cowdenbeath Workshops but at the pits in Ayrshire, Lothians and Fife trying to prevent the growing return to work but by now the writing was on the wall and the strike was lost. Pickets were still mounted but more in desperation than hope. As the return accelerated the frustration and demoralisation grew and those on the picket line, who had sacrificed so much, given their utmost for the cause, withstood police brutality and court injustice, knew that they had been defeated and all that was left was to find some way to return with dignity.

In the course of that twelve long months they had endured an experience they would never forget. They had travelled the country to mount the picket lines at pits, steelworks, factories, coal depots, railways stations and Ports. They had faced the police, the riot shields, the dogs and horses, the lorries and buses which threatened to run over them, as they tried to block the way of 'scab coal' and 'scab buses'.

Many a time they stood there in rain, hail or snow, fired by a determination not to give in, no matter the personal cost, and in the end they could not win. Young men who had entered the struggle with naivety and a sense of adventure were forged in the heat of battle to maturity, learning political lessons about the kind of society they lived in, where the whole power of the state, the police and the courts could be deployed to defeat workers seeking only to defend their jobs and their communities.

Their perception of British Democracy would never be the same again, but they can look back with pride on how they fought for a cause that was right, and no doubt in years to come they will reflect back to the Great Miners Strike of 1984, telling their children of how it was, and over a pint with those who stood shoulder to shoulder with them, recall their favourite tales, sad and homorous, of life on the picket line.

CHAPTER 8

ACTIONS INCOMPATIBLE WITH MY POSITION IN MANAGEMENT

I include this part of the story not because I want to claim any credit for my involvement in the Strike, but because I was in the unique position of being the only member of the Coal Board Management in Britain who was disciplined for publicly supporting the miners' cause. In no way did I ever face the terrible problems which confronted the mining families, but in terms of the local history of the Strike my experiences were quite unusual and significant.

It was not a new thing for me to run foul of my bosses. Indeed it was almost the inevitable climax of the long-running problems I had with them, arising from activities as a well known Communist, a Town Councillor and Parliamentary Candidate. For almost 25 years I had been in this rare position of being the only known Communist in management, which in reality was only possible in a nationalised Industry, for no private company would put up with it, especially if you have been criticising them in public.

My colleagues could never appreciate how someone would jeopardise their career in this way, because it was made absolutely clear for years that there would be no further promotion for me until I mended my ways. Indeed on numerous occasions I was offered the opportunity 'to make a fresh start' somewhere else in the British coalfields in a higher position. I chose not to move - I liked my way of life in Cowdenbeath.

Unfortunately it was not just the Coal Board who instigated several inquiries into my activities. On one occasion it was no less than our local MP Willie Hamilton who prompted an investigation into the allegation that the only people who were recruited into the Workshops, when I was responsible for that function, were Communists. Hamilton was a bitter anti-Communist and raised the issue with the Coal Board Chairman, leading to an analysis of who I had recruited. As it turned out, after a thorough investigation I was cleared completely, as the Board recognised that Hamilton had his personal and political reasons for pursuing a smear against his Communist opponent in the General Election.

I should say that of all the political people I have met, of all parties, Hamilton was by far the most obnoxious, lacking even civility to his opponents. There was certainly no love lost between him and I, and for him to stoop to this level did nothing to improve our relations.

However, I have to say that it was not only the bosses who were uneasy about my being in management. A number of workers did as well. They found it difficult to shed the notion that to be a Communist, you had to be a manual worker or unemployed. I was a long way from the image of the older generations of Communists like Bob Selkirk, Willie Sharp, Rab Smith and others who represented the Party in the area. They were used to Communists as pit delegates, union leaders and councillors, but a Communist in management - no way!

By way of explanation for this apparent contradiction I should say that I was born in a Communist household in Airdrie, Lanarkshire. My father, as a result of being a local leader in the 1926 General Strike, had been victimised and never worked again until the outbreak of the 2nd World War, so I was brought up in poor circumstances, in a home where both parents were dedicated Communists and political activity was a way of life.

My mother was also a very proud and independent person, and like every parent wanted her children to have a better life than they had, so I was encouraged to 'stick in' at school and go to night school for qualifications. Having done well I was identified as having potential and finally landed up in management. Never-the-less I never abandoned the lessons of my childhood and my Communist commitment which led me into the difficulties I have described. However by the time the Coal Board realised who they had promoted - it was too late to get rid of me!

The 1972 Strike, the first National Strike for many years was a particular period of uncertainty for me. The miners were on strike, I supported them publicly but had to go to work. It bothered me so much I consulted Mike

McGahey, the Scottish NUM President, a family friend and fellow Communist. He gave me short shrift, but really only told me what I already knew *'Look, Alex'* he said, *'You cannot stage a one-man Management Strike. All that would happen is that when the miners go back to work after the strike, you would be unemployed. How does that help the miners? So whatever your feelings, we don't need useless sacrifices. So you'll just go to work, and do what you can outside to help the cause'* - That was that - he was right.

When the 1974 National Strike came along, I was more fortunate, as a result of the miners action Ted Heath called an Election and I was the Communist Party candidate for Central Fife. So I spent the time off work campaigning in the Election - with a result that didn't mean a change of occupation for me! In the event the miners recorded a tremendous victory, and the Tories were out. During the course of the election I appeared several times on television in Election Programmes, and it must have been an annoyance to my Coal Board bosses to see me arguing the miners case at every opportunity.

However the miners victory was a lesson learned by the Tories. It was the spur which made them begin to plan their strategy for the 1984 Strike, a strategy which succeeded beyond their wildest dreams, and more than evened the score for the miners victories in 1972 and 1974.

My own position at work got worse after the Tories gained power in 1979 and the climate of industrial relations changed dramatically. All the worst elements in management came to the fore. Following a stormy clash with my bosses, arising out of the Steelworkers Strike in 1983, where Cowdenbeath Workshops was alone in stopping the flow of steel, (despite assurance by Scargill to the steelworkers that no steel would move throughout the coalfield), I was accused of being party to the Cowdenbeath situation, and as a consequence moved to a less contentious managerial job - thankfully.

At least I wouldn't have to deal with those Communist delegates like Jimmy (Colonel) Hynd who often gave me a rough time - so that was a bonus!

When the 1984 Strike broke out, I was once again in this difficult position, but as before I made my support for the miners absolutely clear. I spoke at public meetings, alongside Mick McGahey, George Bolton, Willie Clarke and other miners leaders, raised funds, wrote to the Press, paid a levy to

CHICAGO TUMBLES

On the march down the High Street, Cowdenbeath Rally – August 1984 – headed by Alec Falconer MEP, Gordon Brown MP, Mick McGahey and Peter Heathfield (Gen. Sec. NUM)
(Pics: Courtesy of Dunfermline Press)

the Strike Fund, and helped in every way possible. The minibus of the boys football team that I managed, and which was supported financially by the Workshops men, was put at the Strike Committee's disposal, and I have no doubt it's presence at demonstrations, rallies and picket Lines did not go un-noticed. However, I took the greatest possible care within the premises not to be seen doing anything at work, which could invite trouble, but outside I was clearly backing the miners cause.

Mr Martin, the Works Manager was furious at this, and I don't suppose his superiors were too pleased either, but they were unable to pin anything on me at work, so it was a 'cold war'. On top of that of course I had three sons out on strike, who were 'front-line pickets' and their activities were another source of annoyance to Martin, who would have sacked me immediately at the slightest excuse. There was certainly no love lost between us, and I found him to be totally dishonest in his dealings.

I recall not long after he came to Cowdenbeath, Eddie Garvie the COSA Union delegate and I were discussing how to deal with him, Eddie finally said *"Look Alex, we'll just have to do with him as he does with us - smile to his face and stab him in the back"*. However, we couldn't bring ourselves to come down to that level and he and I were in constant conflict from the day he started till the day I walked out the door - redundant, and anything but voluntarily.

The event which brought it all to a head was a Mass Miners Rally which took place in Cowdenbeath on Saturday 18th August. There was to be a march down the High Street with a meeting in Central Park, the ground of Cowdenbeath FC. The main speakers were Mick McGahey, Denis Skinner MP, Gordon Brown MP, Alec Falconer MEP and Peter Heathfield, the NUM General Secretary. At the time I was Chairman of the Community Council, and two days before the event I wrote to the local paper urging the local people to turn out to support the miners, ending with the emotive slogan *'Victory to the Miners'*. On reflection not the wisest thing to do, however well-intentioned, but passions were running high at the time.

The rally was a huge success, with around 3000 demonstrators braving the rain behind the Dundonald and Dysart Pipe Band, marching to the park and treated to stirring speeches from the leaders. Actually for me it was the first occasion when serious doubt arose that the Strike could be won. I was sitting in the stand next to George Bolton, Scottish Vice-President of the NUM, and asked him how he thought the Strike was going. He paused a moment and then with an all-knowing look said *"Well, Thatcher can't afford to lose, Alex'*. His comment said it all for me. I realised then that Thatcher would use every weapon at her disposal, all the might of police, the courts, the whole power of the state, whatever the cost to the country, to defeat the miners. It was crucial to her whole anti-trade union strategy, and there would be no prisoners in this struggle.

I should have understood this earlier, as some others did after the 'Battle of Orgreave' which was a major defeat for the miners. Despite their continued resistance and apparent optimism, those who experienced that day, realised that they faced a ruthless enemy who would stop at nothing, and in their heart of hearts felt they faced eventual defeat.

However, the Monday morning after the rally I was met at work by Mr Crane, the Scottish Regional Controller of Workshops with whom although we often didn't see eye to eye, I had a good relationship based on mutual respect. He enjoyed a reputation when Works Manager as being 'hard but honest'. You never needed to wonder with him who was wielding the knife when you were being disciplined. He laid it on the line, but honestly. This was in stark contrast to his successor, the afore-mentioned Tom Martin, who I would never have believed even if it was only telling me the time!

Anyway Mr Crane told me I was summoned to Coal Board Headquarters in Edinburgh, where I was to be charged with 'actions prejudicial to the interests of the Board'. I made a quick phone call to my Union President, David Paterson, who was located there. However he was also a Production Manager for the Coal Board, and even as we spoke I could feel him distancing himself from me and reckoned he was a doubtful asset when it came to the crunch.

In the event when I got to Edinburgh he had clearly been in discussion with the Board's senior officials, and it looked as though a deal had been done. I was taken to an office and confronted by Mr Alexander the Area Chief Engineer, the Staff Manager and one or two other officials including Mr Crane. I elected not to have my union representative present at that stage, but to await the charges. Mr Alexander opened by saying that there had been various complaints from the public that I had been seen going in and out of the Strike Centre, and then he produced a copy of the Central

Fife Times, and asked if I had written the letter contained in it. I said *'Who's name's at the bottom of it'*, he said *'Yours'*, and I replied *'well I wrote it'*.

He proceeded to open up a whole line of questioning about my views and activities, but I interrupted him to say *'Look, there's no need to try and find if there's a Red Under the Bed. I've always made it clear I fully support the miners. In this dispute I think they're right, and I will do all I can, outside work of course, to help them'*. He then accused me of being disloyal to the Board, declared that my activities were *'incompatible with my position in management'* and that they were taking action against me pending further enquiries. At this point, prior to sentencing, I asked for the reluctant Mr Paterson, my union representative.

On his arrival I was declared suspended until further notice, I protested at *'their denial of my rights in a democratic country to freely express my opinion as a citizen'* (a little bit tongue in cheek) and denied their right to suspend me. However, Mr Paterson ushered me out of the room in haste, advised me to accept suspension, which would be with pay meantime. Reluctantly I agreed, under protest, and walked out the door, free for the next three months to do as I pleased. Of course I had mixed feelings. On one hand I was out of the Workshops and wouldn't have to pass pickets. On the other there was a good chance they would come up with something on investigation, and I would be on the dole eventually. To be honest, some of the things I had been doing were a bit dicey!

If they thought that suspending me was resolving a problem, they badly miscalculated. At a time when the battle for public opinion between the Coal Board and the miners was intensifying, my suspension was counter productive. Instead of removing me from the scene they projected me into the limelight. When the news got out it made television and radio news. It was carried in the national press, and was the headline in the local Central Fife Times alongside my photograph.

The leading article attacked the Coal Board, there were several letters complaining about the attack on democratic liberty, and even the editorial criticised the action, declaring that it *'reeked of desperation'* at the Coal Board's failure to break the Strike in Fife. Indeed it argued that their action would revive interest in the Strike and harden attitudes. Certainly in my view they shot themselves in the foot. I suppose they had cause to be annoyed, but they should have recognised there were far bigger issues at stake than what I was able to do in the strike, which was very limited, and had no bearing on the outcome. Indeed Mr Crane told me later that he had scorned the suspension as *"it only gave me more time to cause mischief"*

Perhaps Bill Crane picked the wrong description of what I was likely to do but the fact was that apart from the things I was doing openly I was in regular contact with the Scottish, Fife and local leaders of the Strike, and

Picketing the Workshops (Alex Maxwell's house in the background)

throughout took part in discussions on the strategy and conduct of the Strike and how to build public support for the miners cause.

Also I was writing leaflets and press adverts on behalf of the Strike Committees, in response to the Coal Boards propaganda onslaught. I was also helping with transport for the Strike Centre. Apart from the football minibus being used by the Strike Committee I had an old Ford Cortina car, registered in my name, which my sons used in their strike duties and not always wisely!

Unfortunately the registration number began to appear too regularly on the daily report sheet which was transmitted to Coal Board Headquarters in Edinburgh, and I had to ditch it quickly - although I bought an old Lada to take it's place, and asked the boys to be a bit more sensible over what they used it for - but they weren't!

Again although I couldn't picket myself, my house was next to the gates of the Workshops and when there were mass turnouts, the pickets sat on my doorsteps and in my driveway, with the police upset that they were unable to move them as they had my permission to be there. Sometimes my wife laid on tea and sandwiches for the men who were our 'guests'

Indeed I recall a mass picket of about 300 miners around Christmas 1984, when confronted with a hundred police, the miners retired to the Strike Centre leaving only two lads at the blazing brazier at the Workshops gate surrounded by police. Seeing these two lone pickets I decided to fill a couple of glasses of whisky, heat a couple of mince pies and proceeded to waltz my way with my tray above my head, through the ranks of the police to wish the pickets a Merry Christmas and drink their good health. Needless to say that didn't go down too well with the local Police Inspector and his men and if looks could kill I would have been speared to the Workshops gate. That **was** mischief!

During the Strike, whilst most of my activities were open and public, nevertheless, as can be seen some of them had to be carried out secretly as indeed they went beyond merely 'making mischief,' and were undertaken with the clear intention to help the miners side defeat the Coal Board. At the time the truth was in fact that the Scottish NCB officials were correct in their view that my *'actions were incompatible with my position in management'*. Their problems were firstly to prove it, and then to decide whether it was to their advantage to sack me at that stage in the Strike.

In the event the suspension lasted three months, for which period I was paid, and I spent the time helping as much as was sensible in the circumstances aiding the Strike. The Coal Board duly carried out their investigations, which consisted of questioning the people I worked with, individually, if they knew of anything I had done at work, either to influence people to go on strike, or to dissuade those on strike from coming back. They asked if at any time I had ever used the Board's facilities for any of my outside interests, and indeed my next-in-command was asked if I had ever attempted to recruit him to the Communist Party.

It was a typical McCarthy-type witch-hunt, but they drew a blank. They came up with nothing - nobody would spill the beans for they knew my job was on the line, and thankfully they had enough respect for me and for themselves, not to say a word. They could have shopped me, of course, because like most folk, from time to time I had used my employers' time and facilities for my outside interests, but they didn't.

At last after three months I was called back to Area Headquarters. I was met there by Mr Alexander again, but this time it was only him and I, behind closed doors, which made for frank discussion.

His opening shot was to tell me, regretfully, that they had completed their investigations and had come up with nothing. *"You have a very loyal staff, Mr Maxwell"* he said *"No-one would confess to knowing anything about what you were doing"*. He asked me if I knew the nature of the investigations and I said I did. I went on to say that I knew the Board wanted to sack me, and he confirmed that. He said that indeed they had taken legal advice on the sacking, and had been advised that they would lose an Unfair Dismissal case, but *"it would have been worth the £20,000 it would have cost to get rid of you"*. However, it was not the money that bothered them but the public reaction. *"You seem to be a big fish in a small pool in Cowdenbeath"* was his comment, and at this stage they were trying to win the battle for public opinion, so I just wasn't worth the bother.

Nevertheless, he went on to tell me that I could benefit from *'extra generous redundancy terms'* if I wished to go, an offer I turned down. He scoffed at that saying *'so you are one of these people with principles'*. My reply was pretty sharp and sarcastic *"I'm sure you find that difficult to understand, Mr Alexander, - but yes. I like to sleep easy at night, to be able to walk down Cowdenbeath High Street and look people in the eye. It might seem incredible to you, but what I value most is my own credibility, and you can't buy that. So I'll just start back at work tomorrow again, and hope the strike is settled soon"*. He was not at all pleased, but I couldn't care less, and I returned to work, albeit reluctantly, to endure the rest of the Strike.

However, the reaction was to come later, when the strike was over and the miners defeated, and at the first opportunity I was forced out the door, not the least bit on 'voluntary redundancy' with not quite the 'extra-generous redundancy terms' I had turned down - but with no regrets, and a relatively clear conscience.

CHAPTER 9

WHIT DID YOU DAE IN THE STRIKE MUM?

"The hall held four or five hundred people and was packed, mainly with women. Women were going to the rostrum to speak, about the groups they were organising, about the money they were raising, about the kitchens they were running, about the picketing they were doing. These were women who had never spoken in public before; the atmosphere was electric..."

In these words Cathie Cunningham from the Cowdenbeath Strike Centre, described the scene of an unprecedented event in mining history as women from all over Scotland gathered for a rally in Lochgelly Centre in late May 1984, coming together in support of their striking husbands, fathers and sons.

In the Miners Strike of 1984/85 a new stage was reached in the long history of industrial disputes in this country. For the first time the women of Britain's mining communities, the wives, mothers, daughters and sisters, who so often in the past had suffered in silence while their men had struggled publicly, began to form an organised network of resistance in their own right. Women's Support Groups, Miners' Wives Groups, Women's Action Committees, call them what you will, in 1984 their role was vital, and in some cases, essential to the continuance of the strike itself.

In the past, the role of the miner's wife had been subservient to that and that of her husband's. In the early days, during the darker history of the industry, women and young girls had laboured underground, often unpaid, at the side of the men, hauling the coal to the surface several times each day, before returning home to fulfil their 'real' duties as wives, mothers and virtually unpaid skivvies to the men of the household.

Traditionally, the miner's wife had always been there to help sustain her husband in times of hardship. During the great strikes in the early years of this century, in 1921 and 1926, women had been heavily involved in support of their husbands. But theirs was in practice a secondary role. They staffed the soup kitchens and in some cases raised much needed funds. During the shorter strikes of 1972 and '74 they hardly ventured beyond the kitchen. The 'real' strike work, the picketing, fund raising and marching on rallies and demonstrations was the almost exclusive domain of the miners themselves. All this was to change come 1984.

Women on the march in Edinburgh

It was to be the Strike where the women found their collective voice. Women's role in this dispute was to be of paramount importance, not just in the home, but on the streets and the picket lines, where their concerted support for their husbands and sons, would do so much to sustain them during the long months of hardship. Indeed in many cases, it was the women who took the initiative. They organised daily life, both at home and within the community and it would be no exaggeration to say that without the active involvement of the women the strike would not and could not have been continued as long. It was not uncommon, in many households, where, at the outset of the strike, the husband had had to convince his spouse of the need to take industrial action, by the end of the dispute the situation had reversed itself and it was the wife who was insisting on no return to work.

In the town of Cowdenbeath, it was largely through the determined efforts of some of the more enlightened members of the Strike Committee that a Women's Support Group was formed and developed into the force it undoubtedly became. The Group was actively encouraged to take part in all activities concerning the Strike Centre, almost from the beginning. So much so that, come the half way stage of the strike, Cowdenbeath Women's Support Group were not only participating but taking a leading role in many field, both local and national, from fund raising to picket duties. When 'Involve' (the Journal of the Volunteer Centre) covered the Fife coalfield in September 1984, interviewing some the the Women's Groups there,

"We found ... a community solidarity - not in support of the miners as such but in defence of the communities under threat. ...for the informal sector of volunteering, life after the strike may never be the same again..."

This seemed an accurate prediction, as far as a great many women were concerned. The article continued,

At the Cowdenbeath Miners' Welfare, eight women volunteer for five hours a day, seven days a week, running the Strike Centre Canteen. They serve 200 meals at a time to miners and their families. The food itself is donated, or else purchased by means of cash donations.

When the Strike began, a decision was taken by the members of the Strike Committee to attempt the formation of a Women's Support Group in Cowdenbeath. Initially, it has to be said, a few of the committee voiced reservations about the idea, but nevertheless, it was given the go ahead.

There were some women at the Strike Centre already who had volunteered to lend a hand in the beginning. Heather Wilson, whose husband, Gordon was running the Soup Kitchen, Lorraine Adams and her sister Doreen Meldrum, the daughters of a miner, and Liz Bowman. All four were unemployed at the time and apart from their desire to help the miners' cause, they felt that this voluntary work would give them something tangible to do in their spare time, - the only thing surplus on the dole! All confessed at a later date that none of them envisaged the extent of their future activities during the Strike, nor indeed that is would last so long.

The Miners' Welfare in Cowdenbeath had been chosen as the Strike Centre, its Lounge, which could hold 200 people, being used as the feeding area for those who came to the soup kitchen, as well as being the venue for regular meetings, both public and committee. The committee meetings were not always harmonious. Many and varied were the discussions and disagreements, not the least of which concerned the role that the Women's Group should play in the activities. *"Feeling were mixed, ...what you found was that the men liked the women to be involved **up to a point**. It's alright for other men's wives to be involved, but not their **own** wife....*
.....there are men like that. When you think about it, they'd never had to be in the house with the children before, doing the domestic thing. It was also strange for us. It was a step up for us ....

Cathie Cunningham

At the instigation of the Strike Committee, however, a notice was pinned to the notice board, asking for women volunteers. Cathie Cunningham, whose husband Harry was on the committee, and had begun attending the Centre since taking maternity leave from her job as a bank clerk, was the first to sign her name on the board. Lorraine Adams and Doreen Meldrum quickly followed suit. Others, however, were not exactly falling over one another in the rush to sign up, for a variety of reasons.

Certainly not all the reservations about a Women's Support Group were on the part of the men. The women themselves were fairly reluctant to get involved at first. The vast majority had little or no experience of this type of organised activity previously and naturally were unsure whether there was anything they could contribute which would benefit the campaign.

Eventually, as the result of one of the weekly meetings at the Strike Centre, when Jane McKay of the STUC spoke on the role of women in the Strike some of the women were persuaded to attend a public demonstration in Edinburgh, marching to the Scottish Office. The theme of the march was to be a show of public opposition to *"a return to Victorian values"*, a doctrine so dear to the heart of Margaret Thatcher and her Cabinet.

As recorded in the *'Scottish Miner'*.

They (the women) dressed in the hodden grey of their forebearers who drudged in fields, cellars, docks - and pits, a century ago, to symbolise their protests at what the Tories want to take us back to.

The experience of taking part on that march, followed shortly afterwards by the staging of the Women's Rally in nearby Lochgelly, proved inspirational, consolidating the formation of the Cowdenbeath Group and ultimately that of a further number of such groups within Fife.

"I think these two events really did have a tremendous effect on the women, and the whole thing just took off from there". -

Cathie Cunningham.

None of the women, with the exception of Cathie, had ever taken part in any such activities, either political or otherwise. Nevertheless, from the list of volunteers a committee was finally formed, with Lorraine Adams elected as Chairperson, Heather Wilson as Vice Chairperson and Doreen Meldrum as Treasurer.

This setting up of the Womens Support Group in Cowdenbeath proved to be of critical importance in the Strike organisation in consolidating the ranks of the mining families. However it was clear that this did not happen as some local spontaneous outburst of a 'Women's Liberation' movement, for those ideas had barely touched the women in mining communities. The initiative had come from the leadership of the Strike Committee itself, (despite some internal opposition) who gave encouragement and support to women who had never ever been involved in any such movement.

This approach was in contrast to what was happening in other Strike Centres, as was evident from the reports at the meetings of the ten Women's Groups in Fife which were held at the Dysart Headquarters every Tuesday. At these meetings, also attended by women from the Dundee Relief Committee, the delegates often complained bitterly of how certain Strike Centre leaders virtually ignored the womens role in the Strike.

However the initiative in Cowdenbeath was to be more than rewarded, as the tireless efforts of the women mentioned above, led to a group of some twenty four making a magnificent essential contribution to the organisation of the Strike, and were able to involve about sixty women in total in their activities. When one considers that, in the beginning, several of these women were opposed to the Strike itself, their participation in the Womens Group becomes nothing short of remarkable.

Helen Thomson is one such case. At first opposed to the Strike, she, like thousands of other women caught up in the events of that Spring, was distraught about where the money to pay the household bills would come from. Helen and her husband, a mechanic at the Workshops, were in the beginning reluctant to attend the Centre's Soup Kitchen. Coming from a non-mining background (she hails originally from Perthshire) she admits to having had no political persuasions whatsoever before the Strike. However, Helen found that the more she attended the Strike Centre, the more she became involved in its activities. She began to realise that she was not the only one with problems and indeed, it became evident to her that the other women shared her financial worries.

Offering to work voluntarily in the Kitchen, Helen, eventually took charge of 'operations', when Gordon Wilson gave up the position. As if that weren't enough, she made the time not only to attend many of the rallies but also to take her place on the picket line regularly. In recognition of the tremendous work that she and her comrades in the Women's Group achieved during the length of the Strike, Helen Thomson was chosen as Cowdenbeath's Citizen of the Year for 1985, an award which she accepted on behalf of all the group.

Other women had similar experiences. Unlike Helen, Betty Hynd did come from a mining background. Her father had been forced to move from Glencraig to Yorkshire as the result of a previous round of pit closures. Two further moves faced the family when they got there, again due to closures and transfers. The wife of another Workshops man whose own father (Jim 'Colonel' Hynd) had also been a miner and was the Workshops NUM delegate before taking redundancy - Betty recalled her initial feelings.

"I was really scared to begin with. I'd been involved in a Strike before - as a child - but I'd never been involved as an adult with responsibilities...

I was looking at what I should do, what Jim should do ... I panicked, I really did.

It was fear, real fear until I got to know the ins and outs of the dispute".

Like the Thomsons, Betty and her husband were both hesitant, at first to go to the Strike Centre. When they did eventually attend, in order to get the children their entitlement of free milk that Easter, Betty found few familiar faces there. Despite having lived for the past six years in Cowdenbeath, she admits that she *"hardly knew anybody here"* Not only that ...

"To begin with, the Strike Centre wasn't co-ordinated. They weren't getting round to people, telling them what they could do to help".

Again like Helen Thomson, Betty Hynd found that the more she attended, however unwillingly at first, the more she got caught up in the atmosphere there, until eventually.

To me it opened up a whole new world of friendships ...I looked forward to going there. I had to get involved, for the sake of the kids mainly ..."

She found that actively taking part radically changed her whole outlook on life. Her horizons widened accordingly, and she found herself fund raising, not only on the streets of Cowdenbeath, but in other parts of the country.

"I could honestly say I saw more of Scotland during the Strike than I'd ever done before. Aberdeen, Dundee all over...."

One of her abiding memories is of taking part in a Rally for Women down in Chesterfield...

"That was really something ... there were women there from all over, Chile and elsewhere. Anywhere women were downtrodden. It must have been something like going to a big football match, the atmosphere was tremendous.

I felt, going on the rallies, what really impressed me was the number of non-miners that were actually at the rallies. It wasn't just miners, ordinary workers were there in support..."

Charlotte Lindsay is another typical example of a dedicated group member. Her father had been a foreman in the Workshops and her husband was a miner. The mother of two young children at the time, Charlotte freely admits that the Strike drew the family even closer together. Like so many others she worked tirelessly for the cause, attending rallies and marches, as well as doing her stints on picket duty.

"I'd go through it all again. In some respects it was the best year of my life".

What made these women give up so much of their own, and their families' time, in order to help others survive the Strike? Helen Thomson, when asked this by 'Involve' magazine, was eloquent and forthright in her spontaneous response.

"This is a mining community. A dozen pits have closed in the last 20 years and any more closures would finish us off. We are not prepared to let that happen. Never mind what the newspapers say, if you lived here you'd know exactly what it feels like - that's why the people here want to do what they can to help."

When it came to raising funds for the upkeep of the Kitchens, the Cowdenbeath women had no equals. No stone was left unturned in their efforts to glean as much money as possible from an already generous public. Every weekend, and most days in between, the women were out on the streets with their collecting tins and the famous 'miners' barrow', which would gradually fill up with donations of foodstuffs from passing shoppers. Local shopkeepers would be persuaded (or brow beaten) into, donating raffle prizes or cash and a succession of Jumbles, Sales of Work and 'At Homes' were organised. Anything in fact that would keep the soup kitchen open, was given a try.

Wives on the Picket Line at Cowdenbeath Workshiops

Occasionally however, their efforts were not entirely appreciated by the general public. Cathie Cunningham remembers one occasion when the women decided to do 'upmarket' and, rather than holding one of their usual Jumble Sales, they opted to experiment with a 'Coffee Morning' instead. Accordingly they spent money on advertising the event, booked the hall, baked the cakes and made the coffee. And nobody came! It seems that, even in 1984, the good citizens of Cowdenbeath were not quite ready for such 'highbrow' events!

On another occasion, this time in the Strike Centre, one of their 'At Homes' was particularly well attended and somewhere in the region of 100 people had gathered in eager anticipation of the tea and food that would be on offer. However, someone (who would prefer to remain nameless, even though Lillian Scott tends to be mentioned when the story is retold!) had forgotten all about the two hundred or so sausage rolls baking in the oven upstairs. Consequently, before too long clouds of smoke was seen pouring from the kitchen. Lorraine Adams got the job of informing the ravenous hordes, of the culinary disaster - a thankless task! However, all was not lost and, at the end of the day another £100 went into the funds!

Lorraine features prominently in another legendary tale of fund raising endeavours. One fine summer's day, a group of about a dozen of the women set out on a sponsored walk to the village of Kelty, some three miles away. Lorraine enthusiastically led the way, and for a while, all went well. But it was a hot day, the walk was harder than at first imagined and before long Lorraine, of whom the term 'full figured' would be appropriate, began to feel the effects. Her feet and ankles began to swell, dampening her normally cheery disposition somewhat. By the time the group reached their intended destination they were well worn out. However, the day was not a total disaster - the proprietor of the Goth Public House welcomed the walkers with tea and sandwiches and yet another £100 found its way into the coffers.

Tales of Lorraine and her deeds were numerous. Particularly adept at fund raising, she could always be relied upon to 'invite' (coerce) shopkeepers in the area to put up prizes for raffles. R.D. Pringle's Electrical Shop proved especially generous, and as such deserves a mention here.

Whilst fundraising in the town for the Soup Kitchen was of course an essential feature of their work, the activities of the Womens Support Group went far beyond that. In the course of the Strike they travelled throughout Scotland to rallies and demonstration, with their home made banners and their chants. Several of them went to places like Dundee, Aberdeen, Peterhead and Inverness to address meetings and appeal for financial support. Women who had never spoken in public before discovered their voices because of their conviction to the cause.

Others attended the massive Women's rallies in Barnsley and in London where they lobbied Parliament. Most of them had never been in London before, and came back to say the experience was *'brilliant'*

The women too became involved in the picketing, hitherto the special province of men. First at Tullis Russell Paper Mill, then at the Nellie Opencast site, and later at the Fife Pits and the Cowdenbeath Workshops, adding their presence and their voices to those of the men.

Lorraine Adams confessed at the time to an ambition to be arrested on the picket line. In the early days it was almost a 'badge of honour' among the young pickets to be 'lifted' by the police and charged in court. Later it was a less romantic notion as the Coal Board began to sack them as well. However Lorraine and Heather Wilson eventually managed to get on to a picket line at Seafield. They were all excited as they travelled to the pit to await the 'Scab bus' which duly arrived and flew past the pickets into the pit, to verbal abuse.

Lorraine was totally disappointed *"It was all over in two minutes. I expected we would be heaving and shoving - getting stuck into it! I stood there dumfounded - was that it? I had looked forward to it so much and it was a non event"*. Despite being on numerous picket lines after that her ambition to be arrested was never fulfiled - a matter of eternal regret!

As they gained confidence and awareness, some women became involved in topical issues outside the Miner Strike. Their banners were hoisted outside a new Kirkcaldy Hospital and at a Rally in Glenrothes in support of a campaign to defend the Health Service, and others took part in CND demonstrations in Aberdeen and at Faslane on the Clyde. New horizons had opened up for women who till the Strike had only a passing awareness of political events in Britain.

Equally too they did not neglect others in the Community who needed help, and despite the urgent needs of the Strike Centre, still found time and energy to host a fund-raising event for a local woman who needed an electric wheelchair.

Within all these many happenings there were often humerous incidents which relieved the grim battle for survival, and helped keep morale high, but the women would be the first to admit that life was far from being a bed of roses. With personal anxieties over financial problems ever present, the uncertainty of the future, on top of the responsibilities they faced at the Strike Centre and at home, there were bound to be differences of opinion from time to time.

These could be trivial, but they could and sometimes did develop into something more serious. Minor disagreements turned into major arguments and ill-feeling and petty jealousies manifested themselves from time to time. They came into conflict with one another for a variety of reasons, but mainly because of the stress that each and every one of them lived with throughout the duration of the Strike. Notwithstanding, at the end of the day, they battled on together, side by side, to sustain the mining families who depended on them so greatly for their survival.

Working relationships between the women and the strikers was not all plain sailing either. On one memorable occasion, the kitchen volunteers found certain of the men reluctant when it came to picket duties. Eventually they refused to serve them - *'No picket - no food'* and indeed, left the kitchen to take up the picket duties themselves!

The approach of Christmas, 1984 was a daunting prospect. The trickle of returning miners was beginning to grow and the demands on the men and women who manned the picket lines were increasing daily. Splits were developing within communities throughout the coalfields - *"the very thing that the Strike was originally called to protect"* according to the media. In November, with Christmas looming on the not too distant horizon, the 'Scotsman' sent reporter Melanie Reid to Cowdenbeath to gauge women's opinion of the Strike and what they felt the future held for them

The article compared the situation at Bilston Glen pit in the Lothians where there had already been a large return to work with '*the solid mining heartland of Fife, where the numbers returning could be counted on your fingers*' It goes on '*In the town of Cowdenbeath - where a list of names is posted around the streets*

'*For Sale: the souls of the following people can be bought for £1200*' - *the hatred felt to the strike breakers is intense*'.

The women Melanie Reid spoke to - Anne Kirkby, Helen Thomson and Lorraine Adams, to name but three - were nothing short of honest and direct, when replying to her questions.

According to the Scotsman report Anne Kirby was particularly scathing about the strike breakers. "*We feel very very strongly. They are scabs, just scabs. I just hope the Coal Board have got enough pits left to put them in, because our husbands will absolutely refuse to work beside them.. We will ignore them completely. They have made their choice and they have to live with that choice the rest of their lives*'.

Helen Thomson on the other hand found it difficult to come to terms with a situation where another family in the same street had gone back to work. "*We've been friends with them for years. Our children go swimming together. We haven't come face to face with them yet - but whilst you see some women going up to others and shouting 'Scab' . I'm not like that*".

Presentation Time – the Women's Support Group

Asked about the immediate future Lorraine said *"Christmas is going to be the worst yet. The beginning was bad, but Christmas is going to be worse. But once we get through it we'll go for as long as it takes to win."* Anne's comment was *"We never thought we could survive nine months on Strike. But we are surviving. It's easy for us now, and once Christmas is over it will get easier"*

Helen voiced many a parent's fears when she said *"It's hard for the kids coming up to Christmas. My son says he wants a BMX bike: says it only costs such and such a price. It's a shame because they don't understand. The bairns won't get as much as they should have this Christmas, but they'll get something."*

Despite the harshness of their current plight, the Cowdenbeath Women's Support Group pulled out all the stops to ensure that Christmas would be a time of celebration in the town, not a time of mourning. In response to the Christmas Appeal the Strike Committee had launched, donations of money, food, toys and gifts came pouring in from every quarter in Britain and abroad, from businesses, trade unions, traders, publicans, Clubs and individuals, wellwishers and sympathisers, augmented by collections round the doors of the town by members of the Women's Group and the odd male.

Altogether three Christmas Parties were held in the Cairns Church Hall, with around 250 children attending. Due to the womens hard work they were an outstanding success, and once again in another generous gesture by a local businessman any child needing transport was taken home courtesy of 'Ross's Taxis'.

The huge amount of work involved in the preparations for Christmas, the sorting and packaging of gifts from home and abroad, the identifying of children who qualified to attend, the preparation of food and so on had preoccupied the minds of the women involved for a few weeks, to the exclusion of almost everything else from their minds. When it was all over there was an air of anticlimax, as the women slowly returned to the daily grind of making meals, picketing, attending rallies and so on, with by now the realisation that there was little prospect of the Strike ending in the miners favour.

The women carried on doggedly with their chores, despite the despondency and silence in the Strike Centre which told it's own story of their inner feelings. They were now in the last weeks of the Strike and when the end came with the decision to go back 'without a settlement' it was met with sadness and bitterness, but with inner relief, and hope that somehow they could get back to normal life.

Their last picket duty was to be at the Cowdenbeath Workshops on Tuesday 5th March, as they watched the men-folk trudge back through the Workshops gate for the first time in twelve months to resume their work, whilst they shed a few tears before returning to their homes to count the costs of their sacrifice and start to rebuild their lives. It was over at last!

The role of the women in the Strike had been absolutely vital. Not only had they borne the brunt of maintaining their homes and caring for their families in desperate circumstances through the long twelve months, they had taken part in the running of the Strike itself, in the Soup Kitchen, on the street collecting money, organising events, marching in demonstrations and on the picket line.

No doubt they made a crucial contribution to the effectiveness of the local Strike Committee in running the Strike in Cowdenbeath, and providing for the mining families who were involved. Now the Strike was over, with all that they had done, seen heard and learned, time alone would tell what lasting effects it would have on their lives.

COWDENBEATH STRIKE CENTRE
WOMEN'S SUPPORT GROUP

Lorraine Adams - Chairperson
Heather Wilson - Vice-Chair
Doreen Meldrum (Whisker) - Treasurer
Lillian Scott
Helen Thomson
Anne Kirby
Rose-Mary Nicol
Catherine Cunningham
Charlotte Lindsay
Janice Stark
Janice Russell
Elizabeth Bowman
Rose Hoggan
Sandra King
Sandra Taylor
Bridgette Sullivan
Mary Hotchkies
Carol Ross
Anne Marshall
Mary McKay
Tilda Wilson
Margaret Jones
Betty Hynd
Mary-Ellen Jones

CHAPTER 10

BATTLING FOR THE HEARTS AND MINDS

In a struggle of the dimensions of the miners strike the influence of the media is a critical factor. Throughout the Strike, television, the national press, the local press and the publications issued by the unions and the Coal Board all played their part in influencing the attitudes of the general public, and indeed the strikers themselves.

National television and press were in the main hostile to the miners, concentrating on the scenes of violence on the picket lines, portraying the miners as a riotous mob bent on creating mayhem, with the police as the victims and the 'scabs' as decent men who were exercising their right to work.

Day after day that message was being sent out of the homes of Britain, in a concerted effort to turn public opinion against the miners. The treatment of the Orgreave picket was a classic example of how truth was turned on it's head.

The BBC 5.40 news of Monday 18 June described what happened as follows:-

> *The strikers' blockade was planned like a **military** operation with miners arriving from all over the country. But the police responded with speed matching the 6,000 pickets with thousands of their own forces.*
> *At first police horses tried to shepherd the miners out of the convoy road. The violence reached a new peak as miners surged forward against the riot shields. Police **fought** with truncheons* under a barrage of stones and missiles. By mid-morning the picketing had turned to rioting.*
> *The police hadn't lost ground, but more riot squads were needed as **reinforcements** in the front line **as the pressure increased**. Eventually a*

* References to a relatively innocuous incident in the film in which a policeman on the front line uses a truncheon as the pickets press forward.

senior officer ordered in the mounted police **to disperse the miners**. A gap opened and the forces galloped in.

Police horses are the most feared weapon in the present armoury.

But it's the riot squads that follow up to make the arrests and today on the fields around Orgreave the police became involved in some of the most vicious hand-to-hand fighting of the entire miners' dispute. The attacks on individual policemen were horrific. The police commanders said it was a marvel that no-one was killed. The battle lasted throughout the morning, and in all police made over 100 arrests as the **scuffles** ebbed and flowed...

At all times the police were in control but under tremendous pressure.

There was never anything peaceful about the front line confrontation.

It appeared to be a conscious decision to use any method to stop the coke lorries.

Ordeal at Orgreave.

This report puts the responsibility for the violence on the pickets, with the gallant police purely defending themselves against a riotous mob, forced to use their truncheons in the process.

BATTLING FOR THE HEARTS AND MINDS

It was a complete travesty of what actually happened. As described in an earlier chapter it was the police who inflicted the damage on tee-shirted miners, using riot shields and truncheons, hunting down the fleeing pickets, in a cavalry charge, using horses to trample them down and dogs to savage them.

It was miners who were being kicked and clubbed to the ground - the blood being spilled was that of the miners at the hand of the police. There were scenes never witnessed before in Britain in peace time, and police brutality which has left those who were on the receiving end with mental and physical scars which will never be erased.

Fortunately on this occasion there were other TV programmes, particularly on Channel Four, which, because it was impossible to disguise what was actually happening, presented the other side of the story and gave a truer version of events which counteracted the blatant bias from the BBC. On this occasion they had gone too far to hide the truth, but nevertheless overwhelmingly during the Strike the BBC and the national newspapers were hostile to the miners and the 'gutter press' like *'The Sun'* could not find words vicious enough to describe them.

THE PROPAGANDA WAR

Of course all the propaganda was confined to the national news media. The miners unions issued 'The Miner' at national level and in Scotland the 'Scottish Miner'. Their role during the Strike was to report on what was happening from the union point of view and try to keep morale high among the mining families, by posing victory as just being round the corner, if only they held firm for a bit longer.

In the early days the headlines ran:-

    April 1984 - **'ALL OUT'**

    June 1984 - **'TIME IS ON OUR SIDE'**

    July 1984 - **'WE'RE WINNING'**

    August 1984 - **'FIGHT BACK BUILDS UP'**

Then the message was being modified:-

September 1984 - **'BREAK THROUGH IS IN SIGHT'**

October 1984 - **'IT'S COMING YET'**

Next the emphasis nationally was on strengthening the Solidarity movement.

December 1984 - **'TIME TO MOBILISE'**

'UNITY IS STRENGTH'

'ON TO VICTORY'

The Scottish Miner however also added a warning to the Strike breakers and an appeal to them to re-join the Strike.

It's December headline read - **'HASTE YE BACK TO US'**

By now it was clear that to talk about 'Victory' was unrealistic and a negotiated settlement was the best to hope for. However the approach in Scotland was different from that adopted nationally. In a special issue the Scottish Miner in February the headline was:-

'**YOUR** CASE FOR COAL' making a call to take the miners case to all sections of the Scottish people to mobilise public pressure for a settlement.

Conversely 'The Miner' of the same month was headed:-

PRESIDENT WARNS - DON'T BE CONNED' and Scargill called for the *'Intensification of picketing activity'* as *'the very best way to speed talks along'*.

This strategy had patently failed up till then and with the return to work gathering momentum he was asking for one great push too many. Instead the calls from various areas for an organised return to work became irresistible.

The editions of the Scottish Miner and 'The Miner' as the Strike ended, again confirmed the differences which had developed in the leadership.

March 1985 - Scottish Miner **'HAUD FORRIT MINERS'** headed an article congratulating the mining families and launching the campaign for the victimised miners.

In contrast 'The Miner' proclaimed **'THE FIGHT GOES ON'** and then pronounced **'The Dispute Goes on- The Coal Board Have Won Nothing'**,

BATTLING FOR THE HEARTS AND MINDS

a statement that at the time was astonishing and in the light of events after, a complete misrepresentation of the true situation.

Nevertheless despite that final denial of the reality of the conclusion to the Strike, the NUM papers over the piece played an important role in keeping those involved in the Strike informed of what was happening throughout the country and helping to sustain morale, even if at times they were over optimistic in their presentation. Of course given the generally hostile media they had really no alternative.

Outside Coalboard Scottish Headquarters – just after the strike.

Whilst the Union understandably sought to present the state of affairs in the best possible light to combat the hostile national media, the Coal Board for their part spent an enormous amount of money in the propaganda war. A substantial part of that was the insertion of huge adverts in the national and local press, trying to persuade, frighten or bribe the men back to work.

The first of these appeared in early May 1984.

To keep the record straight
HERE IS THE NATIONAL COAL BOARD'S SIDE OF THE STORY:

The biggest fact staring us in the face is that we have been producing more coal than we can sell. That is why there are record stocks.

The Coal Board is concerned for the future. The size of the market will determine the size of our industry.

At the beginning of last year we were producing 8m. tonnes a year more than we could sell. Since then we have taken out 4m. tonnes of output. This year we propose to do the same.

In twelve months time the industry's output and demand will be in balance. We shall then attach the market to increase sales. Out objective will be a minimum capacity of 100m. tonnes a year.

Last year the number of jobs was cut by 20,000 - <u>without anyone who wanted to stay in the industry having to leave it</u>.

And those who chose to go received <u>the most generous compensation terms ever offered to industrial workers in this country</u>.

Again in the coming year, no mineworker who wants to stay in the industry will be made compulsorily redundant.

And another fact we can't repeat too often - <u>there is no new closure plan</u>.

Despite what you might be told, <u>the industry is not being run down</u>. £700-800m. a year will continue to be invested in sinking new mines and modernising existing ones. This highly-efficient new capacity will replace the hopelessly expensive tonnage we hope to take out. And that will make it possible to compete for markets.

Another bright note for the future is that the Board could substantially increase the recruitment of young men a year from now.

Finally, it is not true to say that the Coal Board have stopped discussions. National meetings have continued with the other unions but the National Union of Mineworkers stayed away. Full consultation will resume as soon as the NUM make themselves available.

**THE NATIONAL COAL BOARD.
RE-SHAPING THE INDUSTRY FOR THE FUTURE.**

NCB

That was followed in June with a letter from Ian MacGregor in June warning them of the consequence of their actions.

A LETTER TO STRIKING MINEWORKERS

Dear Colleague,   June, 1984

YOUR FUTURE IN DANGER

I am taking the unusual step of writing to your at home because I want every man and woman who has a stake in the coal industry to realise clearly the damage which will be done if this disastrous strike goes on a long time.

The leaders of the NUM have talked of it continuing into the winter. Now that our talks with them have broken down this is a real possibility. It could go on until December or even longer. In which case the consequences for everybody will be very grave.

Your President talks continually of keeping the strike going indefinitely until he achieves "victory".

I would like to tell you, not provocatively or as a threat, why that will not happen however long the strike lasts.

What this strike is really about is that the NUM leadership is preventing the development of an efficient industry. We have repeatedly explained that we are seeking to create a higher volume, lower cost industry which will be profitable, well able to provide superior levels of earnings while still being able to compete with foreign coal. To achieve this, huge sums of money are being invested in new equipment; last year it was close to £800 million and we expect to continue a similarly high rate of investment in the years ahead. Our proposals mean, short term, cutting out some of the uneconomic pits and looking for about 20,000 voluntary redundancies - the same as last year. The redundancy payments are now more generous than ever before for those who decide not to take alternative jobs offered in the industry.

However long the strike goes on I can assure you that we will end up, through our normal consultative procedures, with about the same production plans as those we discussed with your representatives on 6th March last.

But the second reason why continuing the strike will not bring the NUM "victory" is this: in the end nobody will win. Everybody will lose - and lose disastrously.

Many of you have already lost more then £2,000 in earnings and have seen your savings disappear. If the strike goes on until December it will take many of you years to recover financially and also more jobs may be lost - and all for nothing.

I have been accused of planning to butcher the industry., I have no such intention or desire. I wand to build up the industry into one we can all be proud to be part of.

But if we cannot return to reality and get back to work then the industry may well be butchered. But the butchers will not be the Coal Board.

You are all aware that mines which are not constantly maintained and worked deteriorate in terms of safety and workability.

AT THE PRESENT TIME THERE ARE BETWEEN 20 and 30 pits which are viable WHICH WILL BE IN DANGER OF NEVER RE-OPENING IF WE HAVE A LENGTHY STRIKE.

This is a strike which should never have happened. It is based on very serious misrepresentation and distortion of the facts. At great financial cost miners have supported the strike for fourteen weeks because your leaders have told you this ...
That the Coal Board is out to butcher the coal industry.
That we plan to do away with 70,000 jobs.
That we plan to close down around 86 pits, leaving only 100 working collieries.

IF THESE THINGS WERE TRUE I WOULD NOT BLAME MINERS FOR GETTING ANGRY OR FOR BEING DEEPLY WORRIED. BUT THESE THINGS ARE ABSOLUTELY UNTRUE. I STATE THAT CATEGORICALLY AND SOLEMNLY YOU HAVE BEEN DELIBERATELY MISLED.

The NUM, which called the strike, will end it only when you decide it should be ended.

I would like you to consider carefully, so we can get away from the tragic violence and pressures of the mass pickets, whether this strike is really in your interest.

I ask you to join your associates who have already returned to work so that we can start repairing the damage and building up a good future.

Sincerely,

Ian MacGregor

NCB
NATIONAL COAL BOARD

CHAIRMAN
Ian MacGregor.

In reply to that an open letter appeared in the Central Fife Times and the 'Scottish Miner'

STRIKE BULLETIN

Miner's Reply to Mr. MacGregor

...."Unlike the vast majority of my fellow workers who burned your letter on receipt, I am taking the unusual step of replying.

"First of all can I say that in no way do I regard myself as your "colleague." My life is bound up with the mining industry and its future. In contrast you have merely been hired, as enormous expense, by a Government which detests the miners, to butcher the coal industry and smash our union.

"When your job is done you will walk away without remorse about the industry, its workers and the mining communities you have destroyed in the process.

"Whatever your assurances, your record in the steel industry is evidence of your ruthlessness in pursuit of your so called business objectives. That same ruthlessness is now being applied to the coal industry and I have no doubt at all of your intention to close 70 pits and get rid of 70,000 jobs. You want to close down the "perpetual areas" like Scotland, Wales and Kent and leave 100 super pits employing 100,000 men which can then be sold off to your friends in private enterprise.

"This is the Tory Government's strategy in every other nationalised industry and we will not escape if you have your way..

"Yes, my future is in danger but only because it is in your dangerous hands.

"In order to realise your objective you have the full backing of the Government who hope to cripple the NUM, traditionally the most militant section of the British Trade Union Movement.

"You have used bribery, blackmail and threats. The Government have tried to starve us back by cutting social security payments and they have given the Police unlimited resources to break us. For miners, freedom of movement has been stopped and we are subject to verification, harassment, intimidation and arrest.

"But you will not succeed. we will not be bribed, conned, starved, or jailed into submission because our cause is just. We are fighting for our jobs, our families and our future.

"The immense damage to our industry is caused not by us, but by you. We want to save pits, not destroy them. The coal industry belongs to the British people, not an imported American businessman, who has no idea how miners live, think or feel.

"Your term as chairman has been a disaster for Britain. You have cost the British people millions of pounds, caused immense damage to our industry and brought our society a frightening level of civil disorder.

"This is not America and your methods and philosophy have no place in our coal industry or our country.

"As you have failed miserably in your present job, and since you are quite happy to advocate redundancy for men half your age, you should have no objection if I suggest than in the interests of our industry and the British people, you should go now."

'Cowden Miner'

The adverts from the Coal Board continued in July telling the miners how they were being 'conned' by their leaders.

HOW THE MINERS ON STRIKE HAVE BEEN MISLED...

ABOUT WHAT THE STRIKE CAN ACHIEVE

The miners on strike are angry. And it's easy to understand why.

They are angry because of what they have been told by their leaders.

But have they been told the truth?

The sad thing is that the only result the strike can achieve is irreparable damage to the industry.

Can the strike stop pit closures?

No - for a very simple reason.

The future of coal depends upon how much it costs to mine. The cheaper it is the more of it we can sell, and therefore the more of it we can mine.

The more expensive it is, the more it will pile up unsold, like the 55 million tonnes at the beginning of this year.

No matter how long the strike continues, it cannot change this basic fact.

We need to replace four million tonnes of our most expensive coal with economically-mined output.

This will bring the average cost down - and allow us to sell more coal from our better pits.

Doing this is exactly what was agreed in the 1974 Plan for Coal - to replace old, uneconomic capacity with new economic capacity.

The final Tri-partite Report on the Plan for Coal said in Paragraph 27, "inevitably some pits will have to close as their useful economic reserves of coal are depleted".

A mere 12 per cent of our capacity is now directly costing more then £275 million a year to support. This is money that should be going into modernising our other pits - as the Plan for Coal hoped it would.

That will safeguard miners' jobs, increase wages, and give Britain the coal industry it needs.

The strike cannot do that. The only thing it can achieve is the very opposite.

If it goes on long enough, the strike threatens up to 30 good pits with permanent closure.

This could not only cost miners, but also steel and railway workers jobs that should not be lost.

Can the strike win new business?

Everyone knows it can't. It is driving away future coal customers.

It is making coal more difficult to sell.

It is threatening the future of the industry.

Britain is the only country in Western Europe that is investing so heavily in the future of coal.

The British coal industry has excellent prospects.

But not if the strike continues.

This strike - not the Coal Board - could butcher the industry.

That's why it is so important that this strike ends soon.

It was called by the miners' leaders. It now needs to be called off by the miners themselves.

NCB
One in a series issued by the National Coal Board.

In August the message was that the Union were refusing to compromise, and appealed to miners to break the Strike and join *'the growing number of returners'*

WHY THE TALKS BROKE DOWN...

THE NUM HAD NOTHING TO OFFER.

The last talks between the NCB and the NUM ended in deadlock on the 19th July with no date fixed for a resumption.

In an effort to provide a basis for a return to work, the NCB volunteered to meet some of the NUM's demands but only if the Union would agree to certain NCB conditions.

Miners ignored by their own union.

The union offered no concessions at all and even chose not to consult their members about terms of the NCB's 'package'.

The issue that caused the breakdown was their refusal to accept that financial losses could ever be a reason for closing a pit that still had some coal reserves left.

They repeated their claim that the Board were breaking Plan for Coal. Yet that document says "inevitably some pits will have to close as their useful economic reserves of coal are depleted".

Neither the NCB nor the NUM can ignore the reality that the whole country has far too long paid the bill for keeping hopeless pits open.

But the NCB understand the impact on people and communities. So they offer alternative jobs to men who want to stay in the industry when their pit closes. And for those who leave, redundancy terms which are the best in the whole of Western Europe.

The Coal Board believe that this industry can have a great future, <u>but we have to create it ourselves through improved performance - and this can be done with no hardship to anyone.</u>

A steady return to work

More than 60,000 people are still working in the industry. Every day their numbers are increasing.

They realise the coal industry offers them a prosperous, secure future.

If you are a mineworker why not join them/

NCB
The National Coal Board

By October, bribery was the ploy, with promises of substantial redundancy pay-offs

YOU DECIDE.

DOES THIS SOUND LIKE AN INDUSTRY BEING 'BUTCHERED'?

Coal stocks were 53 million tonnes at the beginning of the year. The NCB proposed to reduce coal production by 4 million tonnes excess capacity and to adjust the workforce by a combination of natural wastage and voluntary redundancy.

Best redundancy terms in Western Europe.

Men who wish to leave are being offered a lump sum of up to £36,000 if under 50. Older men received a smaller lump sum plus up to £104 a week until the age of 65.

Nobody forced to leave

Alternative jobs in other pits are being offered to men who want to stay - with generous transfer allowances and other benefits. There will be no compulsory redundancy.

A new enterprise company financed by the NCB, will provide every possible help in attracting new businesses into the local communities. So, despite what you've heard, the industry isn't being butchered or people thrown on the scrapheap.

Efficient coal production now will safeguard thousands of jobs in the future.

The Board is investing upwards of £800m annually to secure that future.

THE NATIONAL COAL BOARD. NCB
SHAPING THE INDUSTRY FOR THE FUTURE

At Christmas the emphasis was on the benefits of returning with an offer of 'safe passage'

NCB
SCOTLAND

More that a quarter of Scottish Miners are now back at work.
Coal will be produced again at Bilston Glen, Monktonhall and Barony Collieries at the end of the New Year holiday.

Regular wages are now easing months of hardship for thousands of Scottish mining families.

If you have given enough of your time and cash to the strike and want to get back to work - Here's a promise from the National Coal Board.

1. Your wage packet for week starting January 7th can total up to **£140**. Wages for the following three weeks will give you up to **£560** and allow you to qualify for **£255** holiday pay for the summer break of 1983/84. **It is unlikely that you will have to pay any tax until the end of March.**
2. Your future employment is guaranteed.
3. Immediate consideration of all requests for voluntary redundancy.

We can make arrangements to bus you into work and help make sure of the safety of both you and your family. Clip the coupon and sent it to

N.C.B., FREEPOST, Edinburgh, EH17 0NQ if you want us to help you get back to work.

```
Name..............................................
Check no. .......................................
Address ..........................................
```

This information will remain confidential.

In January again the accent was on the crumbling of the Strike and the advantages of being back at work

SINCE WE LAST SPOKE TO YOU, ALMOST ONE-THIRD OF ALL SCOTTISH MINERS ARE BACK AT WORK!

Since we last spoke to you, there has been a considerable move back to work. From a quarter to nearly a third of the entire Scottish workforce, in fact.

1. Coal is currently being produced at Bilston Glen, Monktonhall, Killoch, Barony and Seafield.

2. Almost **4,000** men are working. That's over **30%** of the NUM membership in Scotland.

3. If you go back right now, you almost certainly won't have to pay Income Tax until the end of March.

4. We guarantee you future employment.

5. And we'll give immediate attention to all requests for voluntary redundancy. If that's what you want.

Your future, your family's future, and the future of the coal industry is in your hands.

NCB SCOTLAND

Until this time the NUM had not used the press in the same way to reply, but in Fife at a meeting of leading figures in the Dysart Strike Centre, it was felt that there was a need to combat this continuous propaganda, and issue a message to the Strikers and the general public with the call for a 'negotiated settlement'. I agreed to draft the advert, and shortly afterwards another on the same lines and these were published in all the Fife newspapers.

NUM DYSART STRIKE CENTRE

A MESSAGE TO THE PEOPLE OF FIFE
WHO IS PROLONGING THE STRIKE?

Since we last spoke to you over 95% of Fife miners have remained on strike in defence of their jobs, their pits and their communities.

In spite of NCB propaganda, the miners have stayed loyal to their Union even if after 11 months on strike, they suffer poverty and hardship. No other men and women have endured so much - and remained steadfast.

THERE MUST BE A NEGOTIATED SETTLEMENT
TO THE PEOPLE OF FIFE WE SAY:-

Continue your support for the miners - but demand an end to Government interference and the resumption of negotiations.

This strike can only be ended by a honourable settlement. We have sacrificed too much for too long to surrender now.

And yet the Tories persist on trying to starve us back to work. The NUM want to settle this strike by negotiation and so do most of the NCB Management.

All sections of the British public, including the Churches, are also urging negotiations.

NO PRE-CONDITIONS FOR TALKS - SAY THE NUM

ONLY THE GOVERNMENT OPPOSE AN AGREED SETTLEMENT

The NUM have made it clear they will enter negotiations without pre-conditions - leaving room for the wide-ranging discussions.

But the Coal Board, under government orders, wanted written pre-conditions they sit down at the negotiation table.

They still believe they can break the strike by a drift back to work.

It is a fact that every miner who returns to work now is helping the Government and delaying the resumption of talks.

THE GOVERNMENT IS TYING THE COAL BOARD'S HANDS

However they denied it in the past, everybody can now see clearly it is the Government who are stopping the settlement. From the start they set out, not to tackle the problems of the Coal Industry, but to destroy the NUM. They have used bribery, intimidation, the Police and the Courts. They have cut Social Security and wasted £5,000 million of public money to break the strike - and they have failed! But still they pursue their vendetta against the miners, no matter the damage to the economy, reflected in the plunge of the poind to an all-time low and the bitter divisions in our society.

The tories are trying to achieve the impossible - to smash the NUM - and the British people are paying dearly for it.

IT IS THE GOVERNMENT WHO ARE PROLONGING THE STRIKE FOR POLITICAL PURPOSES

TO OUR MEMBERS WE SAY:-
Stand firm - no return to work until we all go back with an honourable settlement - including our members who have been sacked.

TO THE PEOPLE OF FIFE WE SAY:-
Continue your support for the miners - but demand an end to Government interference and the resumption of negotiations.

SETTLE THE STRIKE NOW - BY NEGOTIATIONS!

In February the Coal Board came back with their final push. The huge adverts combined the themes of the Strike failing, the threat to the industry, and the redundancy money just waiting to be collected.

This is what **working miners** have

GAINED

by going back to work in the Lothians and Ayrshire

1 Resumption of coal production at Bilston Glen, Monktonhall, Barony and Killoch Collieries.

2 Deliveries of their own concessionary coal.

3 Repairs to their pits to make them ready for production.

4 The start of a training programme for young miners.

5 Tax free wages and holiday pay.

6 Voluntary redundancy terms for 500 men who wanted to leave the industry with lump sum payments in some cases of more than £30,000.

7 A return to normal family life.

This is what **striking miners** have

LOST

by NOT going back to work in Fife.

1 The loss of more than 800 jobs following the underground fires at Frances and Seafield.

2 The loss of key coal faces at Castlehill Mine in the Longannet complex.

3 Minimal repair work being carried out to get the pits back into production.

4 No apprentice recruitment and training.

5 An average loss of wages of more the £7500.

6 Voluntary redundancy only available to those men who have returned to work.

7 Continuing family hardship.

More than **1000** Fife miners know what they have lost and have returned to work. They are joining more than 70 per cent of the workforce who have ended the strike in the Lothians and Ayrshire.

Your future, your family's future and the future of the coal industry is in your hands.

SCOTLAND

By this time it was clear to even the most diehard striker that the Strike was lost, that there could be no negotiated settlement, and that unless the end came quickly those on Strike could end up in a minority nationally. It was time to return if the Union itself was to be preserved in any meaningful way - the return to work without a settlement was on the cards.

Looking at these adverts once again, in the light of what has transpired since those times, with the assurances that they contain about the future of the Coal Industry and how people would be treated, it can be seen that the phrase *'economical with truth'* would be a grossly understated description of their Coal Board authors.

'DEAR SIR' - LETTERS TO THE EDITOR.

The propaganda war was not of course confined to the main contestants at national level. Historically the local paper *'The Central Fife Times'* had long been a forum for debate on all kinds of issues. Indeed the circulation of the paper was influenced greatly by the number and quality of the *'Letters to the Editor'* and I recall 'Old Bob' Selkirk, my respected predecessor on Cowdenbeath Town Council telling me that if circulation was declining the Editor himself would pen a provocative anonymous letter, knowing that this would set in motion a chain of correspondence to entertain a waiting readership.

Whether that is true or not I'll never know, but looking back on some of the anonymous contributions published I am highly suspicious. However, the Strike itself produced many letters to the press, a sample of which show how the battle of ideas was being conducted locally. Once again those who attacked the Strike mainly wrote under nom-de-plumes, recognising that the views they expressed were by no means popular.

The first critic appeared in the guise of 'Another Democrat' following an appeal I had made in the Centre Fife Times for help, donations and food for the 'Strike Centre' and for the community to rally around the miners.

"What a disgrace to tell miners to claim social security benefits and free school milk for children. Other industries are having to close, so miners like others will just have to face the facts of life" (CFT.29.3.84)

Then there was an attack on the Labour Party by 'Ex-Miner' who said *'that in 11 years in power, Labour under Wilson and Callaghan had closed about 330 pits, and 90 closures in 9 years by the Tories was tame in comparison*

'Disgusted' added to this attack by condemning the local Labour Councillors in particular Mike Judge, who was due for re-election *'he has never yet said he supports the miners. Instead of genuinely supporting the miners these people seem to me just trying to get votes all the time'* (CFT 19.4.84) That was a bit uncharitable as Mike's only crime had been to appear on the High Street with a collecting tin!

'Democrat' re-appeared to condemn the actions of the pickets, but 'Miners Picket' retaliated by quoting the abuse of police powers *"Telephone tapping, the use of agent provocateurs, random and mass arrests, political interrogation, police violence, road blocks. I've seen it myself, Democrat doesn't know what he's talking about - so shut up!* (CFT. 19.4.94)

J. Hunter from Lochgelly added his piece *"Democrat indeed, With friends like that in a mining community - who needs enemies"*.

'Onlooker' was the next opponent to enter the arena claiming that the money being collected on the street was being misused *'Would the public be so generous if they knew where the money was going? Could it be that the biggest expenses incurred are for hiring buses and giving spending money to the pickets?"* (CFT. 10.5.84).

Jimmy McGavin from the Lochgelly Strike Committee replied by inviting 'Onlooker' along to the Centre where *"we will offer him the opportunity to inspect our finance'*(CFT.17.5.84) Needless to say the offer wasn't taken up by the shy 'Onlooker"

A new line began to emerge in May as the Coal Board adverts appeared offering *'the most generous redundancy terms ever'*. 'Hopefully Redundant" wrote how he had phoned up Seafield and applied *'to get away from all this unrest and uncertainty'* while 'Hopelessly Dejected Miner' exclaimed *"I want out. Everybody is sick fed up, miserable and disgusted. Families are at each other's throats, wives are demented, and at their wits end trying to make ends* meet" (CFT. 17.5.84)

He was followed by 'Disillusioned Miner' who attacked the Scargill leadership and claimed that "many miners, in fact probably the majority, have no stomach for the fight" (CFT.24.5.84)

George Selkirk from Cowdenbeath came back quickly 'it's all right for such people to take the redundancy money and run, but what about the young miners who will find it virtually impossible to get work in this areas". If 'Disillusioned Miner' is going to write letters such as this, please have the stomach to sign your real name' CFT.31.5.84) However, it seemed as though "Disillusioned Miner' had no such stomach, for he never reappeared.

In July there was another flurry of letters from 'Local Boy', "Fed-up Miner' and 'M.McHale-Seafield Miner' against the Strike but a particularly vicious one from 'Hopeful Miner' who vilified "Scargill and his KGB executioner McGahey" who "are hell bent on the downfall of the Government" and "the miner is being used to further their aims". He goes on with a savage indictment of Scargill, then blames a 'Bunch of thugs and gangsters who had driven a poor miner beyond the human endurance to take his life. What was his crime? he wanted to work" After this outrageous claim he makes the quite legitimate call for a ballot, but ends by apologising for using a nom-de-plume "because I am also afraid of gangsters" - presumably striking miners.

Replying to 'Hopeful Miner' Andrew Hood from Rosyth, laid the blame for the Strike totally on Prime Minister Thatcher "Maggie has been at the back of this Strike from the start - she would like to take us back to Victorian days - if they defeat the miners where will they turn next" (CFT.2.8.84)

Also responding was 'Former Miner', Cowdenbeath who declared that "The only real gangsters 'Hopeful Miner' should be afraid of is the mob from No.10 Downing Street who have brought havoc on so many of our industries and made life so pointless for so many young people".

The notorious Willie Hamilton MP of Royalty fame then entered the fray, his first words in five months into the Strike made not to support the miners but to undermine them. In a speech in the House of Commons he said that *the Strike had gone on too long to do anybody any good"* – "pits would close regardless of the Government in power, and there was no point in trying to make political capital out of an inevitable geological fact. He believed that the vast majority of miners secretly wanted to get back to work as they were 'down on their uppers'

His statement was greeted with derision, as a stab in the back from an MP who had long lost his 'Sell-by' date and was soon to be challenged for re-selection in his Central Fife Constituency.

'West Fifer' from Lumphinnans seemed surprised that he had spoken at all about the Strike *'The only thing we ever heard from him before was his dislike for the Queen'* whilst Richard Whyte was for extreme measures *'Re-selection? he should be strung up from Lochgelly Cross'* although 'Old Timer' though that *'hanging's too good for him - he should get a kick on the ——'.* (CFT. 9.8.84)

From then till the end of the Strike Willie Hamilton was conspicuous by his silence and absence and indeed he was removed as the Labour candidate for Central Fife at the next re-selection conference. Not a lot of tears were shed at that, and certainly in the years I knew him and contested for Parliament, of all the candidates from every party, including the Tories, he was he most offensive, and we were well rid of him in the Fife area.

'Local Boy' was next to attack. He argued that *'people have the right to work just as much as they have the right to Strike'* and condemned the pickets whilst praising the police. *'It has been witnessed that the police have attended to the injuries of Strikers but not Strikers attending to injured policemen'*. At the same time 'Fed Up Miner' was still trying to organise a meeting of those who wanted back to work *'at the gravel park at the bottom of the Public Park at 11.00am on Saturday,* In the event "about 50 people turned up but *'the vast majority were those in favour of the Strike continuing'* (CFT. 9.8.84)

'Local Boy' now indulged in a little crystal ball gazing. After writing that a 'Miners Wife' should *'be rejoicing that as collieries are being closed down less men will have to go down the pits, consequently health-*

ier men will be walking the street' he goes on to say 'there is absolutely no logic in clinging on to pits that are outdated, dilapidated and uneconomic' and proceeds 'rest assured there will be new and better coal mines opened up'.

Well, the new coal mines haven't materialised so far, and even whether the who've lost their jobs are walking the streets healthier is debatable. There's certainly a lot more of them walking the streets - unemployed and left to waste.

At the end of August these was a flurry of correspondence and editorial comment about my suspension, in the main very critical of the Coal Board for what they saw as an attack on civil liberties. However, 'Concerned' from Cowdenbeath concentrated his criticism on the now familiar theme of picket line violence.

'The man who stands on a picket line peacefully has nothing to fear. the police only turn out in accordance with the number of pickets. - which has a new definition, kicker, stone thrower, unlawful occupier of property, beater up of fellow Trade Unionist, who happens to dare to think, let alone think differently. If the police were not present it would be miner murdering miner in the name of Union solidarity'. (CFT.13.9.84)

I replied to this one myself in the following vein, suggesting that in fact we were witnessing almost the creation of a police state:-

'We now have what is in effect National police force, employing the most sophisticated equipment to monitor all movement of miners. Freedom of travel is prevented, road blocks are established and miners are treated like criminals. We have seen police on horseback hunting down miners like animals across the fields using dogs to intimidate pickets, and lining up like Roman soldiers with riot shields and truncheons to charge into picket lines of miners in tee-shirts, bumpers and jeans.

It is the police who arrive on the picket lines prepared for violence and spare no effort to escort a few scabs through picket lines'.

Referring to the high number of arrests I said 'You don't have to do anything to be arrested - you just have to be there or even just on your way. The police make their own laws or dig up an ancient one when they can, and woe betide the miner who tries to argue with them Equally too, when miners appear in court massive fines ranging from £300 to £750 are imposed for 'breach of the peace' until now a minor offence. All of this is the use of the police and the courts to intimidate and defeat the miners'. (CFT.20.9.84)

By now George Erskine from Lochgelly was getting a bit fed up with the anonymous snipers and ridiculed 'those worms who write from under the stone of anonymity' pointing out in the course of his letter 'this town was built on the blood and sweat of miners in the past. Now that their descendants are fighting for the survival of their jobs the working people cannot turn their backs on them'

A new nom-de-plume then arrived in the shape of 'John Doe' who claimed that 'the right to work (for those who wanted to break the Strike) is a precious thing and he hadn't met a single miner who didn't want to go back to work'.

Iain Chalmers from the Cowdenbeath Strike Committee replied to agree with him 'that no one I know of in the Industry wanted to Strike, including myself — but I will not go back on the Coal Board's terms which 'mean a 50% cut in coal mining capacity' By going on Strike we are doing something. We are in a struggle to protect our jobs. Yes Mr John Doe, the right to work is a precious thing - a right the NUM and it's members will fight for, a right that nearly 4 1/2 million have been deprived of – THE RIGHT TO WORK (CFT.13.9.84)

By October many families were suffering badly and this prompted a local poet to make this contribution to the paper in verse, whilst expressing the continued resolve not to give in.

The Miners' Lament
My TV.s gone, my video too,
   My life is all in a dither,
My car's untaxed, my wages is axed,
   And the wife is haveing anither.
Ive burnt all my fencing and two of my chairs,
   I'm just about near off my heid;

> Early this morning, we went into mourning,
>   Noo oor wee budgie is deid.
> The bairns are howling about poor wee Billy,
>   It makies my heart fairly bleed,
> But what can you do when pennies are few,
>   I canny even buy seed!
> We're scrimping and scraping tae make ends meet,
>   We do without this and that,
> I feel line a sinner when after oor dinner,
>   There's nothing left for the cat.
> We're sat round the fire burning a tyre,
>   Trying to make a bit toast,
> We keep it alight for part of the night
>   Wi' the Mail and the Sunday Post.
> Oh I wish it was all settled up,
>   But I know that somehow I'll stick it,
> I'd rather eat grass than try ever to pass.
>   Thru' the ranks of a miners' picket.
>
> Ben Giraldas.

In November there was by now a major drift back to work in other parts of Scotland but not yet in Fife. However, our ever 'Hopeful Miner' was still anxious *'to go back to work now and settle this stupid dispute'*

Once again there was an invitation to *'any man who thinks the same to meet at the red gravel Lochgelly Park on Friday at 11 o'clock.* He had as much success as the previous occasions, although it seems that other miners were busy elsewhere on what seemed more worthwhile.

'Grateful Pensioner' at least had a good word to say about them *'I believe there should be appreciation for the young striking miners who every day cut up logs of wood and deliver in bags to us old people. They don't restrict the longs to miners, retired miners and widows but deliver to many old folks outside the industry. Thanks lads for helping us keep warm* (CFT. 25.10.93)

'Disgusted Miner' echoed what a lot of people felt about the failure of Kinnock and the Labour leadership to give public support for the miners. In contrast to Local MP's Gordon Brown and Dick Douglas who identified themselves with the miners cause, at national level Kinnock was careful to distance himself from the miners because of *'picket-line violence'*.

The letter writer said *'His (Kinnock's) reaction when asked at the Parliamentary Labour party to give public support to the miners was 'that he did not want to be tied up with a glorious defeat'*

(CFT 15.11.84)

With Christmas coming up 'Robin Thomson' wrote to say he was 'going to try to get to work before the 19th to get the Christmas bonus of £650. I think we have got a good deal out of the NCB. Let's go back to work now. Get in contact with your pit to get transport on the 12th. (CFT. 15.11.84)

But 'Auld Has Been' urged men to resist what were paltry sums compared with their future earning potential, giving examples. He said **Naturally the sums of money offered are very tempting to people who have struggled on through an eight month strike. But surely no miner who has suffered will entertain such a gullible piece of propaganda, without at least giving it a thought'.** (CFT. 15.11.84)

Iain Chalmers too entered the columns to answer 'Hopeful Miner's call to return to work by emphasising the devastation facing mining communities as a result of pit closures. He used a finishing line which was to strike home with the Strike breakers. **'Christmas isn't going to be easy, but it's only one Christmas. I may be hard-up now, but I won't always be hard up. But a scab will be a scab forever'** (CFT.8.11.84)

'Old Blue Eyes' was another who urged the miners to resist the blackmail and bribery from the Coal Board as Christmas drew near. Warning them against the cost of 'scabbing' he said **'the price for their Christmas dinner is too high for any decent man, and they will rue the day they scabbed. The miners went out together and they should go back together when the Strike is settled and not before'** (CFT/22/11/84)

Alongside these there were other letters, all anonymous, attacking the strikers, praising the scabs, and urging a return to work.

'Housewife' talked about **'the once proud miner - with his begging bowl in his hand'** - **'the brave few who dare to go back to work - living in fear of violence'** and **'it's high time they got back to work before they drag our country down and further.**

'Disenchanted Donater' complained that the money being raised was being misused to pay pickets ' **£2 a time every time they travelled on a bus, 20 cigarettes every time, breakfast and lunch'** and the Strike Committee members in the Strike Centre **'always sitting with** their pint glasses filled' 'The decent miners never go near the Strike Centre'.

To complete the trio 'Onlooker' returned once more to his theme of picket violence and the terrorisation of 'decent miners'. 'I know who will get the sympathy. It will not be the thugs, but the men who can brave the threats and decide enough is enough'. (CFT 29.11.84)

James O'Hare (decent miner) made the reply denying all the smears and the allegations of misuse of funds and concluding 'All I can say is that you are another of the silent majority who want someone else to do your dirty work. I take it your middle name is 'Yuk'.

The drift back to work was arrested for some time as Christmas arrived but the letters to the Press did not slacken. 'Old Miner' sneered at Scargill and returned to the 'failure to ballot' mistake 'Where does he lead them. Into chaos violence and anarchy. And who pays the price, the poor suckers who follow their leader into misery widespread hatred and want'

'Observer' claimed that there was a 'silent majority' who had been denied their democratic right to vote 'But all they can do is watch the working miner stand up for his rights' - 'while his otherwise mates say to one another - 'I wish I had his guts' (CFT 6.12.84)

'Fifer' didn't quite see the working miners as the heroes that 'Observer' did. What he saw was a 'a handful of scabs slinking out of their homes, into their mobile cage, gathered by a posse of sneering snarling overpaid Thatcherites (we used to call them policemen).

Keith Hynd (a proud striking miner) 'described the Strike "as a struggle' for the right of every working man an woman to have work' and appealed to the anonymous critics to 'stand up and support the Miners struggle for if we are beaten there will be no place to run from the Thatcherite regime' (CFT.6.12.84)

The following week a letter from Sean O'Neil from Belfast also emphasised the importance of the winning of the Strike and urged 'all Fife workers to unite, stand firm, and stand and be counted now' - Your dispute is international all whose who believe in freedom, democracy and socialism are watching and waiting in hope'

A little nearer home 'Striking Miner's Daughter' also put the emphasis in holding on keeping hopes high in this piece of verse:-

Don't Quit

When things go wrong
As they sometimes will,
When the road you're trudging seems all uphill,
When the funds are low and the debts are high,
And you want to smile, but you have to sigh,
When care is pressing you down a bit-
Rest if you must, but don't you quit.

Life is queer with its twists and turns,
As every one of us sometimes learns,
And many a fellow turns about
When he might have won had he stuck it out.
Don't give up though the pace seems slow-
You may succeed with another blow.
Often the goal is nearer than
It seems to a faint and faltering man;
Often the struggler has given up
When he might have captured the victor's cup;
And he learned too late the night came down
How close he was to the golden crown.
Success is failure turned inside out-
The silver tint of the clouds of doubt,
And you never can tell how close you are,
It may be near when it seems afar;
So stick to the fight when you're hardest hit
It's when things seem worst that you mustn't quit.

'Striking Miner's Daughter'

It was a message of hope for Christmas and well intentioned but most people knew it would need a Christmas miracle to change the desperate situation. However Santa Claus would still visit the miners children that year by courtesy of massive help from home and abroad. Donations of toys, food and money came pouring in, but even that generosity did not please the phantom letter writers.

'Central Fife' wrote 'I strongly object to the door-to-door collection for Funds for the Striking miners Children's Christmas fund. It is the miners themselves who are denying their own children a happy Christmas by not returning to work. 'When one goes to the Strike Committee they are always to be found in the bar with drinks and cigarettes - where is the money coming from? No one is starving, and all are prosperous looking' (CFT.13.12.84)

However the Christmas parties were a great success, with over 250 children attending, because of the many donation from people who didn't share the view of 'Central Fifer'.

Christmas over, and back to the daily picket grind. By now there were sufficient people back at the Cowdenbeath Workshops to justify this letter from 'Paddy the Picket'

'Day by day more and more lorries driven by scab drivers are leaving the workshops with equipment bound for private companies. These lorries are being loaded by striker breakers who are betraying their mates and putting everybody's job in jeopardy including their own.

Once the work goes to private firms they will never return, and by their actions the scabs are helping to close the workshops, not save it'(CFT. 19.12.84)

This claim proved to be only too true as later events unfolded.

The drift back was still limited in Fife but the phantom pens continued their work. This time it was 'Another Realist' who claimed the strike was all a Communist plot 'The evil today in Britain is the Communist Party which has slowly over the years been eating into Britain's industry and lifestyle. Scargill was just the front man they needed' then after urging a return to work he concluded 'ten months is a long time to be on strike, but it does not mean that you fight till you are dead. Being dead helps no one'(CFT.12.1.85)

From then the letters began to taper off, because really there was little left to say that had not been said before. It was clear that the miners could not win and it was only a question of whether any kind of honourable settlement could be achieved.

'Pensioned Off Miner' wrote 'I wish the striking miners the success they are seeking for a reasonable settlement and jobs for all. Long live the miners (CFT. 16.2.85)

However as Jim Hardie replied 'The truth is that the NCB and the Government do not want a negotiated settlement. The NUM is ready and willing to negotiate with no pre-conditions. They are not willing to give an abject surrender' (CFT. 28.2.85)

It was only too true the Government wanted nothing less than unconditional surrender, and a week later the men went back 'without a settlement'

Just previous to that AS Jamieson penned a little poem hoping that the two main opponents could get together to 'kiss and make up' The last verse ran-

> 'Pleased to meet you, glad to know you,
> There are joys for us to share
> For the future beckons to us
> Take my arm and we'll get there'

It seemed to me at the time a rather pious piece of wishful thinking after twelve months of bitter conflict and so it turned out.

The miners who had given so much for so long, fighting for their jobs and communities returned to work with McGregor vowing they would *'pay the price of insurrection'* and he was more than as good as his word.

Looking back over all those letters to the Press, it was apparent that those hostile to the Strike chose to write anonymously. Whilst many people criticise people who won't publish their names below abusive letters, nevertheless I think they had real cause to worry about the reaction from strikers if they exposed themselves.

Given the hostility to 'scabs' which is shown in mining communities, they did run a real risk of at least verbal abuse as they went about the business. In truth not all of what they said was wrong. There were examples of violence against scabs. There should have been a ballot. Scargill did see the strike as a great political crusade against the Government and persisted in wrong tactics.

But by far the main victims were the striking miners, at the hands of the Coal Board, the Government, the Police and the Courts. Their cause was just they were fighting for their industry, their jobs and their communities, at tremendous sacrifice to themselves and their families.

How many anonymous writers there were we don't know perhaps only one or two using different nom-de-plumes, but whatever their expressed concern for democracy and the right to work, it is clear that they were opposed to a strike from the start, no matter the scale of the Coal Board closure plan and it's consequences for the mining families.

One critic who was not anonymous, however, was the local minister the Rev PC Rae and he too was opposed to the Strike. He conveyed that message early in the Strike in his *'Thought for the Week'* column in the press in this way:-

> "Yet even today men are tempted to strike, to destroy, to be rebellious
> surrendering to temptation and hence sinning. Drive out sin and Satan,
> stop the rebellion by believing the word of God".

(CFT 22.3.84)

Unfortunately the Lord himself apparently was one of the few who chose not to air his own opinions through the columns of the Letter pages - unless of course he sent them under a pseudonym!

CHAPTER 11

SCABS, SUPER-SCABS – AND OTHERS WHO RETURNED

' After God had finished the rattlesnake, the toad and vampire, He had some awful substance left with which he made a scab.
"A scab is a two-legged animal with a cork-screw soul, a water-logged brain, a combination backbone of jelly and glue. Where others have a heart he carries a tumour of rotten principles.
"When a scab comes down the street, men turn their backs, the angels weep in heaven, and the Devil shuts the gates of Hell to keep him out.
'No man has a right to scab so long as there is a pool of water to drown his carcass in, or a rope long enough to hang his body with. Judas Iscariot was a gentleman compared with a scab, for after betraying his Master he had character enough to hang himself. A scab has not.
'Esau sold his birthright for a mess of pottage. Jusdas Iscariot sold his Saviour for 30 pieces of silver. Benedict Arnold sold his country for the promise of commission in the British Army. The modern strike-breaker sells his birthright, his country, his wife, his children and his fellow-men for an unfilled promise from his employer.
'Esau was a traitor to himself; Judas Iscariot was a traitor to his God; Benedict Arnold was a traitor to his country. A STRIKE-BREAKER IS A TRAITOR to his God, his country, his wife, his family and his class. A REAL MAN NEVER BECOMES A STRIKE-BREAKER....'

This definition by Jack London, the famous author, was made about 'Blacklegs' in a mining strike in the Graw Valley of South Wales in 1929, and whilst nowadays it may appear 'over the top' nevertheless it reflects the loathing which was felt in mining communities for those who stayed at work whilst their fellow workers were on strike, suffering the hardships and poverty that afflicted those who chose to fight in this way to protect their jobs or conditions of work.

Over the years since mining began in Scotland there have been countless strikes, major and minor, and those who broke the traditional solidarity which characterised the miners, and became 'blacklegs' were ostracised at the time and never forgotten afterwards.

I can recall as a boy in Airdrie my father pointing out the father of a school friend of mine and saying *'See him, don't trust him. He scabbed during the '26 strike'* This was at least 20 years after the strike but still he had not been forgotten.

Perhaps my father, as one who had led out steelworkers in Bellshill in that strike, was victimised as a result, and never worked again until the outbreak of war in 1939 was particularly bitter - but I don't think so for, those who take part in great struggles like that, there is little forgiveness for the ones who break ranks.

As in 1926 so in 1984. Even today when my hometown football team Airdrieonians comes to Fife to play voices in the crowd will roar out *'Scabby Bastard'* to John Martin, the Airdrie goalkeeper, who is still reviled for breaking the strike when he was an electrician at Bilston Glen colliery in the Lothians.

He has tried to put a brave face on it, so I can only imagine how he must have felt over the last ten years as he stood between the goalposts, being reminded by verbal abuse that the former miners here have never forgotten his 'betrayal'. Such is the fate of those who choose in times of strike to set themselves apart from the mass of the workers who take industrial action against their employers.

Ten years on from the strike it is easier to discuss objectively why those who went to work did so when their workmates and wives stood outside on the picket line suffering all the privations of a year without wages, although I doubt if even as they did it they realised the lasting legacy of their decision. Certainly attitudes have mellowed in some cases, to those who only gave in nearer the end, but still there will always be a question mark over their names.

SCABS, SUPER-SCABS – AND OTHERS WHO RETURNED

In all forty-seven people returned to work at Cowdenbeath Workshops during the twelve-month period of the Strike (nine of whom actually lived in Cowdenbeath itself) out of a labour force of 325. Unlike the 'Black-list' published by the Fife & Kinross Miners Union in 1892 of all the 'black-legs' at each of the pits in Fife and Kinross, including Cowdenbeath, Little Raith, Lumphinnans, Donibristle, Fordell, Hill of Beath and Kingseat Collieries, I have chosen not to reproduce the full list of the strike-breakers in this strike, and only mention individuals to illustrate a relevant point in my presentation of events.

As written in an earlier chapter, only two men in the Workshops never went on strike at all - George Cummings and Tom Young, both foremen who in fact had participated in the two earlier National Strikes in 1972 and 1974. As was typical of most of the early returners they did not live in Cowdenbeath nor indeed in a mining community. They were the original 'super scabs' and eventually took the first offer of redundancy terms and got out before the strike finally ended.

The Coal Board of course developed a strategy for breaking the Strike. They identified those who lived outside the recognised mining communities, those who had never been strong union members, and those who were 'not too bright', and made concentrated efforts to entice them back. After the first 3 months when there was no real movement back to work, Martin the Works Manager and Hunter his willing accomplice analysed the work force and began to make phone calls or write letters, on top of the massive Coal Board propaganda.

However, it is interesting that contrary to expectation, it was not poverty that drove the first people back. For example Billy Williamson at the Workshops was one of those who went back early, although with the agreement of the Strike Committee he had been working quite regularly maintaining the Emergency Winder and being paid – although he was reluctant to hand over the agreed levy to the Strike Fund.

He was the first Cowdenbeath resident to break the strike and certainly he and his family suffered the consequences, with his house windows broken frequently and he subjected to verbal abuse. Billy played football with a local Junior Club, Lochgelly Albert and on occasion a group of strikers would turn up as spectators and subject him to continued harassment. To this day the hostility has not ended.

John Hoggan, a very competent Inspector in the Workshops was another who went back early on, but again not because of hardship. John was a man who was reckoned 'not to be short of a copper' but never a strong union member. He had a strange attitude.

I can remember going round dropping leaflets through doors in the town asking for money for the strikers children's Christmas Appeal. Pushing a leaflet through one particular door I was confronted by John. Like other strike-breakers by now he lived in fear that his home would be attacked and he was obviously agitated. I explained what I was doing at his door and he sighed with relief and then offered a donation to the Appeal Fund! I politely refused.

Another early returner was Wattie Henderson from Dunfermline.
Wattie's personal attributes made him an ideal target to be persuaded to return to work. Before the Strike Wattie was the 'fitba' coupon' man in the workshops, But when he broke the strike many were the plots to waylay him on his way to work and teach him the error of his ways. However, the plots never materialised, but after the strike, Littlewoods must have noticed the fall in his sales!

Other were less fortunate. Jimmy Graham, a lathe operator from Lochgelly had his car and house damaged by angry strikers and others lived in fear of damage to themselves and their property.

As time went by a small number of men with whom I had good relations before the Strike, went back to work. Sam Perkins an electrician who I had played golf with at Workshops outings, 'Dally' Duncan a turner from Bowhill, who had been a Communist Party sympathiser, Ralph Tunstall, a painter who decorated my house from time to time, John Ferguson, the foreman mechanic who repaired my car on occasions. At work we crossed paths on a daily basis. But we never discussed the strike, nor indeed ever spoke a word to each other. The uneasy silence itself spoke volumes.

The strain on the 'scabs' was immense, as they faced the daily ordeal of passing their former workmates on the picket line. Some of the strike breakers could hardly stand it. One man, Les Harper, in fact was about 'flipping his lid'. When he came back to work he went about the

SCABS, SUPER-SCABS – AND OTHERS WHO RETURNED

Workshops with a hard-hat with 'SCAB' painted on it in white letters. We used to play a game daily around the clocking rack. I made a practice to note the numbers at work and kept the Strike Centre informed. He would try and catch me doing it. One day he hid in the nearby toilet to surprise me in the act and then confronted me in rage and ranted on. I said *"Look Les, you should remember one day this will all be over and the boys will be back - so don't be so stupid"*.

For my pains he reported me to Hunter the Superintendent, who sent for me. Whilst I despised what Hunter was doing to break the Strike, we had previously had a friendly relationship and he finally decided not to take it further. It was a close call, because if Martin the Manager had found out, I was away!

In my job previously I worked closely with the Shop Foremen, and as the strike carried on beyond six months an increasing number of them returned. Young and Cummings of course had never gone on strike, and Jimmy Greig was among the first to join them but they were eventually joined by others. Near the end people such as John Hutton from Kelty, a popular foreman, Derek King from Thornton, Wattie Glancy from Cowdenbeath and unfortunately one of the most respected foreman of all Arthur Rae from Kirkcaldy, a first class engineer and hitherto held in high esteem.

It was very difficult for me as they resumed work, as I had always had been on good terms with them, but I have no doubt it was even more difficult for them. I'm sure the ordeal took it's toll on them, and certainly Arthur Rae was never the same again. Like the others he got out of the workshops soon after the Strike, and we never met again until we both attended the funeral of a former Union Branch Treasurer in the Workshops called 'Nobby' Clark. Arthur looked so wearied I felt compelled to go and speak to him and shake his hand - like some others forgiven but not forgotten.

As indicated the Coal Board kept up a constant stream of propaganda in the national and local press to persuade or bribe men into returning to work, with ever new attractive financial packages on offer, including the suggestion of an opportunity to get good redundancy terms if they wished.

At local level the team of Martin and Hunter identified those who they thought could be persuaded back to work and made selective phone calls or wrote letters to them. Peter Watson 'Pablo' from Kinross was one of those who responded on the basis of assurances that there would be large group coming in on one particular Monday. He duly arrived, to discover he was the only one to take up the offer, much to his great annoyance, but the deed was done.

In Cowdenbeath itself there was no organised return by the strikebreakers themselves, until well into the dispute. A meeting was arranged at Beath High School of a group who wanted to go back to work, but in the event only a few including Tom Arnott, an electrician and Canteen Manageress Yvonne King actually did. After the Strike, Tom Arnott was made the foreman of the department.

The others who attended the meeting apparently decided it was not the wisest thing to do and changed their minds at the last minute, some even as they arrived at the top of the road to the Workshops and saw the pickets.

Armoured 'Scab' bus passing pickets at Frances Colliery. (Pic: J. Beall)

When there were only a handful of strikebreakers at the beginning, they came to work by car. At first the pickets at the workshops gates attempted to reason with them but to no avail. The first to ignore the pickets and

SCABS, SUPER-SCABS – AND OTHERS WHO RETURNED

race through with his car at high speed was Ian Laing, an electrician and he was lucky to escape without real damage to his car as he did so. From then the police were required to protect the cars of those who went through as arguments sometime gave way to more physical methods of 'persuasion'

At a later stage when the drift back began in earnest around October, the Coal Board arranged the transport in the form of buses, by courtesy of a firm called 'Parks of Hamilton', a name loathed throughout the coalfields, equally with the haulage firm of 'Yuill and Dodds' who roared through lines of pickets all over Scotland, transporting coal at the height of the strike. Both these companies were detested by the striking miners and to this day their very mention is guaranteed to produce language not fit to be printed in this book.

The scabs working day began by them gathering at a selected pick-up point, (such as at Fordell Training Centre or the local Police Station), which would change whenever the strikers discovered the location. The time, too varied to try and baffle the pickets as well, but there was always someone outside the gate to meet them in the morning and see them off at night with a barrage of verbal abuse.

The pickets had an old hut built at the workshops entrance. It was called 'The Alamo' and the pickets kept themselves warm with a fire in a home-made brazier. Whilst it was named in a spirit of fun, perhaps it was a prophetic choice. The battle of the Alamo resulted in a massacre of the defending forces by the Mexicans, and whilst no blood was shed at this 'Alamo' the final outcome for the strikers was also a total disaster.

As the number of 'scabs' increased towards the end so did the pickets. A hard core of twenty would be augmented by a hundred on occasion and on one occasion four hundred pickets confronted the police. The drill was the same each day. The buses would arrive at the head of the street leading to the workshops, and as they moved down the road the occasional person would hurtle abuse. The buses were camouflaged to hide the owners name, the windows were barricaded with steel mesh and the 'scabs' cowered down or turned away their heads.

The vehicles were a sinister sight as they drove through the Workshops gates past the line of pickets, men women and sometimes children who gave vent to their anger by shouts and screams. I doubt if even the hardest 'scab' could fail to be affected by the sight of their fellow workers, wives and youngsters suffering the poverty and worry that the long struggle had brought.

Inside the Workshops, they were warmly welcomed by Martin, the Manager and Hunter his enthusiastic lieutenant, with handshakes and encouraging words. In the beginning they did almost nothing, and spent the day generally cleaning up or comforting each other. Later they did some work, and indeed loaded plant on to lorries to take it out to those pits which had re-started. But of course the Coal Board weren't concerned whether they worked or not. That was not the issue. They weren't there to produce anything -they were merely tools to break the strike.

At the end of the day they were reluctantly shepherded on to the bus, each usually carrying a small bag of coal, and were patted on the back and sent on their way by the smiling Martin and Hunter. Seldom have I ever seen such a pathetic sight, and I felt really sick at this daily ritual. Once again they were driven out through the picket line in their armoured bus and returned to the assembly point. Sometimes they were trailed by striking workers, not just to the dispersal place, but behind their own cars to their homes, and no doubt they would be more than a little apprehensive in those circumstances.

In the main the strike breakers avoided any confrontation with the pickets and seem more shamefaced than anything else, but Yvonne King the canteen lady who lived in Cowdenbeath was particularly nasty and there were heated verbal exchanges both on the picket line and in the High Street when she ventured shopping there. This continued after the Strike and eventually she sold up her home and moved on.

The striker breakers were very conscious of my presence in the Workshops, and knew full well they would be unable to conceal their identities. Indeed the Strike Committee were informed of every one who was at work, so that they could monitor the situation and perhaps persuade some of them to re-join the strike. Approaches were made to some of them with success.

An extract from the Committee Minutes of 20th November 1984, reproduced opposite illustrates the attention being given to the 'scab' situation.

20/11/84 Chairman F. Kirby.

E. Garvie reported that the bus transporting scabs into the w/shops, was operating from the car park next to the police station in stenhouse street.

Anti Scab Activities
Possibility of high street public demo.

Make up posters and placards.

It was noted that the scabs presently in the w/shops are as follows G. Gollan J. Graham T. Arnott L. Elder S. Perkins I. Laing W. Henderson D. Young P. Watson Y. King W. Williamson T. Brown L. Harper G. Cummings J. Ferguson T. Young B. Davidson T. Greig J. Sinclair K. Bowman A. Proudfoot. A. Johnston.

Anti Scab letter
E. Garvie submitted the letter to go to every member. It was agreed to hang on until great letters frankonly. it was endorsed by the committee and it was hoped they could be delivered tonight.

T. Allan reported that J. Sinclair had requested two union representatives to visit him tonight. It was agreed that J. Hardie and F. Kirby undertake this visit as it was felt this man would rejoin the strike.

Although in the cases shown in the minutes the approach was unsuccessful, there were indeed some men who were persuaded to re-join the Strike. Those who had weakened momentarily were welcomed back to the Strike Centre - forgiven if not entirely forgotten, as it turned out later.

The attitude of the strikers to the 'scabs' was of course bitter. Each new strike-breaker was a weakening of the ranks. Men who they had worked alongside for years were seen to be traitors, friendships were destroyed, never to be restored, and so too with the wives and families of those involved.

No question as the strike progressed there was intense hatred of those who went back early. They suffered continual verbal abuse, and sometimes physical attack and damage to their homes and property. They couldn't visit their usual pub or club, they could hardly be seen out shopping or walking the streets of the town. They were outcasts, often prisoners in their own homes, fearing some reprisal on themselves or their property. Their names were published on lists around the town and painted on the road at the Workshops. It must have been hell!

When the strike was finally over and the men returned, the atmosphere between those who stayed on strike and those who 'scabbed' was acrimonious. There were sections where a single 'scab' would be working alongside several other men and no one would speak to him for weeks on end. They sat at teabreaks alone- outcasts from the normal chaff and banter of everyday life at work, with only their fellow 'scabs' to pass an occasional greeting. They were the butt of sarcasm and malicious pranks.

Now that they had served their purpose the Coal Board Management treated most of them no better than anyone else, and they took redundancy as quickly as possible, no doubt relieved to get away from it all to try and seek normal lives.

Looking back ten years later, how should they be seen, those who for one reason or another, went back to work whilst their mates stayed out to the finally defeated? Were they in the right? Were they only being sensible in a 'no-win' situation? Were they indeed perhaps men of courage who were prepared to defy the 'Picket mob' or were they truly only scabs - those who were traitors to their fellows - who lacked the courage to fight and to suffer for a noble cause?

SCABS, SUPER-SCABS – AND OTHERS WHO RETURNED

Has Jack London in his quotation at the beginning of this chapter got it right or should we be more charitable, and understand their actions? No doubt they committed what has traditionally been regarded as the greatest sin of all in mining communities -to break that solidarity and community spirit with which mining areas have always been famed.

As an individual who did not himself suffer the privations of those who endured that bitter twelve months, although my own three sons were front line pickets and faced real financial difficulties like everyone else, it would be presumptuous for me to seek to pass judgement on the 'scabs' I am not in a position to make such a judgement. In life most of us never have to face such a test of character and resolve, and we may react differently from what we think.

Perhaps we should consider the argument that it was the policy of the national leadership, in failing to accept a compromise agreement at critical stages in the Strike when that was possible, and continued to pursue an unwinnable objective, that made scabs out of many good loyal union men in the final weeks of the Strike.

Indeed one South Wales leader in those last few weeks concerned about the long term survival of the Union, as *'good men were unable to maintain their loyalty after nearly a year of sacrifice'* urged the leadership to *'call it a day'*. He put the issue bluntly in this way to them *'To prosecute this Strike to the bitter end we have seen our members become 'Beggars', we have seen them become 'Criminals'; we should not allow them to become 'Scabs'.*

There has to be validity for that view, as the logic behind continuing the Strike further as Scargill sought to do was indeed to make 'scabs' out of more and more of those whose sacrifice was almost total, and destroy the Union entirely. In many areas indeed the majority of men were already back at work, with only Fife in Scotland still relatively solid, so fortunately we were spared the deeper divisions amongst the workforce which followed elsewhere.

However after many discussions, at the time and recently, with those who stuck it to the end, the consensus seems to be the same. There were 'scabs' and 'super-scabs', and there were others who went back after Christmas and nine months on Strike, when all seemed lost, that it would be harsh to condemn totally. But the prevailing view remains that *'we all went out together; we all should have gone back together'.*

By that criteria, some of the local strikebreakers will never be forgotten nor forgiven, whilst others will be forgiven but not forgotten. Undoubtedly none of them will ever erase that ordeal from their memories. The experience took it's toll on them and they will be scarred for life. The sad fact is that no matter how good a workman or respected an individual they were before the Strike, the thing they will most be remembered for in later years is that they 'scabbed' during the 1984 Miners Strike. In mining communities that is the cross the strikebreaker must carry, however unjust it may seem in individual cases.

I haven't been able to find out just how they feel now, ten years later. I wonder now with the benefit of hindsight if they think it was all worthwhile, and they would do the same again. But the subject is too painful to discuss as it opens up old wounds, so I can only speculate. However, what I am sure of, is that those who were tempted to join them, but for one reason or another did not, will always be glad of that, and be correctly proud that their names are included in the 'Roll of Honour' reproduced in this book.

For those who failed to qualify for inclusion then perhaps these very simple lines by a young girl from Nottingham, included in a book of children's poems about the Strike will be an appropriate epitaph for most of them.

> "Here lies the body of Billy Dab
> Pity it was he was a Scab
> The pickets stood and called his name
> And finally he died of shame"

Jayne Petney (14)
Nottingham

CHAPTER 12

THE END AND AFTERWARDS

As 1985 dawned there was little hope of *'A Guid New Year to Ane and A'*. To those on Strike, Burns lines from 'To a Moose' would have been more apt. *'An' backwards when I cast ma e'e on prospects drear, and forward tho' ah canna see, I guess and fear'*. It was clear that victory was impossible, and the best that could be expected was some mercy - an honourable settlement which would allow the men to go back with some consolation for their sacrifice.

The picketing continued and so did the arrests and dismissals. The Fife men were stretched to the limit, trying to stem the tide wherever further cracks appeared, but it was a hopeless task, and yet in Fife 90% of men were still on Strike. They hung on grimly, having given so much already, but stubborn in their determination not to succumb.

In some cases it was the women who were the stronger. Women who had opposed the strike at the start, but had been transformed by their experience, threatened their husband of dire consequences if they went back to work. The line was that *'we came out together and we go back together'*.

The Strike Committee did their best to hold the line. Reacting to Press reports that the Workshops was threatened with closure they mounted a mass demonstration there. Also trying to counter the Coal Board propaganda that there was a rush of men back to works and that the strike was collapsing, they produced leaflets designed to boost morale. (an example of one is shown on the next page).

In January and February there were still major rallies and demonstration but now the emphasis of political, religious and union leaders was for a honourable settlement. Their plea fell on deaf ears, and confronted with

COWDENBEATH STRIKE COMMITTEE

Dear Colleague

THE TRUE POSITION AT THE WORKSHOPS

Forget the "Sunshine Stories" in the press about the Workshops. Here are the facts:

1) 43 scabs are in attendance out of 350 employees

2) Half the scabs are foremen, inspectors, storekeepers etc - non producers

3) The place is frozen, the water is cut off daily due to bursts. Working conditions are very bad and there is no union to help the men.

4) Production is minimal. It took 4 weeks to build 8 chocks, despite working weekends and using fitters to build up a squad.

5) Over 700 chocks have been sent out to private enterprise - along with all the spares. So far none have been returned.

6) The mass demonstration forced the Coal Board to issue statements that the workshops are safe - and mount a press publicity stunt.

7) The NUM insist that the workshops remain a viable unit. The NCB must not be allowed to make it into an 'uneconomic' unit by taking away work and cutting manpower.

8) Our pickets monitor all that goes in and out and will continue to do so.

WE SAY TO YOU

We support the call for a negotiated settlement to the dispute, not a surrender to Thatcher and MacGregor's terms.

Let there be no return to work until we can all go back together with an honourable settlement - including the members who have been sacked.

YES WE WANT A SETTLEMENT - BUT BY NEGOTIATION!

Late Extra

There are some who say we could guarantee our future by 'drifting' back to work. But look at what's happening at Newbattle and Lugar who've had far bigger returns than us at Cowdenbeath. The Board have responded to this by laying the boot in further. At these workshops, sections are being closed down, the work transferred to Cowdenbeath and the men given redundancy. 45 have already gone at Newbattle - including men in their thirties, leaving the rest demoralised. This shows that if you lie down - they will tramp over you. If you stand up and fight-they back away. Our long term interests lie in staying united and strong.

UNITED WE STAND - DIVIDED WE FALL

THE END AND AFTERWARDS

the prospect of there being more men at work than on Strike a National Conference of the Miners decided on a *'return to work without a settlement'*

The news that the Strike was over was met with a mixture of despair and relief. Despair that after twelve months of struggle, they were unsuccessful and relief that at least it was all over and life might return to some thing nearer normal.. A final mass meeting was held in the Strike Centre, but with different decisions at some pits as to the date of return, for almost the first time in the Strike there was some acrimony before agreement was reached to resume work on Tuesday 5th March 1985.

On that day the workforce assembled and sadly marched together through the gates past the women who had gathered by the roadside. The Strike was over at last - the men were back, defeated, dejected and in debt. For those who had fought so hard for so long with great courage and tenacity it was tragic, but they went back with dignity, still united, the young men grown to maturity with their unique experience, to face an uncertain future.

With the Strike over, shortly afterwards the Strike Committee met to wind up their affairs. The Treasurer, Jack Allan reported that the Strike General Fund contained £3,907.76p. It was decided to make a donation to the Miners Welfare for the use of their premises, to several other voluntary organisations who had been particularly helpful, and to pay out £10 per head to every striker who was on their Strike Centre Register.

It was also agreed to have a plaque made commemorating the use of the Miners Welfare as the Strike Centre and to present it to their Committee, as well as giving a plaque to each member of the Women's Support Group. These decisions emptied the Strike Fund completely. (see letter over)

Back at work the immediate concern of the Union leadership was for those men who had been sacked during the Strike, but Ian MacGregor in his moment of triumph was anything but magnanimous. At the start of the Strike he had described it as *'a little problem on the other side of town'*. Now he crowed, referring to the men the Board refused to re-employ, *'People will discover the price of insurrection - and boy are we going to make it stick'*

The *'little problem on the other side of town'* was estimated to have cost the

National Union of Mineworkers

Cowdenbeath Strike Centre

Dear Colleague

<u>Disbursement of Strike Fund</u>

At our last Strike Committee meeting it was agreed to make a final payment from the local Relief Funds to each member who remained on strike throughout.

Please accept this £10 along with our best wishes. Can we also pay tribute to your loyalty to your Union and your workmates inspite of the hardships of 12 months on strike.

In our view no other body of men and women could have given such magnificent support to their leaders and we are proud of our members in Cowdenbeath.

Yours sincerely

B. Easton
Secretary.

Government £2367 million, including £189 million on extra payments to police sent to the coalfields. Over 10,000 miners had been arrested, and incalculable damage had been done to relations between the police and the public in every mining community.

Workshops men campaigning against closure – October 1988 (Pic: Courtesy of Dunfermline Press)

In Scotland 1350 arrests were made, and 470 cases came before the courts. 18% of these resulting in 'not guilty' verdicts. There were very few serious charges, most being for obstruction or breach of the peace, but four months later of the 203 miners sacked in Scotland none had been reinstated, unlike their counterparts in England and Wales.

In Cowdenbeath Workshops, Ronnie Campbell, Billy Arthur and Jimmy Whyte had been dismissed for picket line offences, as were Andy Lawrie and Sean Lee who lived in the town. Of these only Jimmy Whyte was ever reinstated.

The atmosphere in the Workshops was awful. The manager was cock-a-hoop with the victory but if the life of a 'scab' was bad enough when the Strike was on, it was almost worse back after it was over, when they had to work beside the very men they had turned their backs on. The atmosphere was bitter, the scorn vicious and the isolation soul-destroying. Most of them found it intolerable and took redundancy at the first possible opportunity.

The fine words of praise they got from Mrs Thatcher at the Lord Mayor's Banquet in London on November 12th 1984 must now have had a hollow ring. *'This has been a tragic strike, but good will come of it. The courage and loyalty of working miners and their wives will never be forgotten'*. Later she reassured a strikebreakers wife concerned about the outcome of negotiations in February 1985 *'there can be no betrayal of the working miners to whom we owe so much'*.

In spite of that reassurance after the Strike, Mrs Thatcher was to take MacGregor to task for his failure to help these very people. He protested that he had done his best *'Many of these courageous men elected to leave the industry and take the generous redundancy terms on offer. We moved many hundreds of the rest to other pits and areas where they might have peace and arranged new housing for them. Thousands more were counselled and helped with their problems'*.

If as MacGregor had vowed that the striking miners would pay the *'price of insurrection'* there was heavy price too for those who 'scabbed' in terms of the reaction by their former workmates. More than that in Cowdenbeath Workshops as elsewhere they were treated little better by the Management for their 'loyalty', having served their purpose. Truly whatever the immediate problems of the returning strikers, they would be overcome, but the 'scabs' were left with little reward and a life-time legacy of betrayal to live with.

The Workshops at Cowdenbeath was soon the last in Scotland as the ones at Lugar and Newbattle closed. But it was blatantly obvious that the future of Cowdenbeath itself was in jeopardy. Work was being transferred to English workshops or going out to private enterprise. With each cut in workload a fresh wave of redundancies took place, and there was no lack of volunteers amongst all but the youngest men.

The demoralisation of defeat, allied to the mountain of debts accumulated during the Strike, was enough to tip the balance in favour of redundancy terms which seemed reasonably favourable, with the hope that maybe a new job could be found somewhere. One of the saddest sights I have ever seen was of men who manned the picket lines for a year, endured poverty so much, waiting in a queue in a passage to be interviewed for redundancy.

Production at the Workshops after the Strike was at an all-time low, as can be expected. The Scottish Chief Engineer, Alexander, and Martin the Works Manager decided that morale could be lifted by producing a Workshops Bulletin. They decided that since I had a talent for writing I should edit it, from materials submitted by different members of management. I guess they suspected, rightly, that I had written some of the local Strike material, and I think they were trying to rub salt in the wound.

Anyway we produced a glossy magazine called *"FOCUS"* and it was distributed to the workforce to much ridicule, given the way that work was being off-loaded elsewhere and the Workshops run-down.

The introductory message alone shows how much the content was worth. A day or two after, another one page paper named *"FUCUS"* was distributed that commented on what the management were up to. The fact was that the Editor of both documents was one and the same, although I had to coarsen the language to try and disguise the fact. Martin knew alright but couldn't prove it. The Paper is reproduced here and despite it's crudeness accurately describes the process that was going on in the post Strike days.

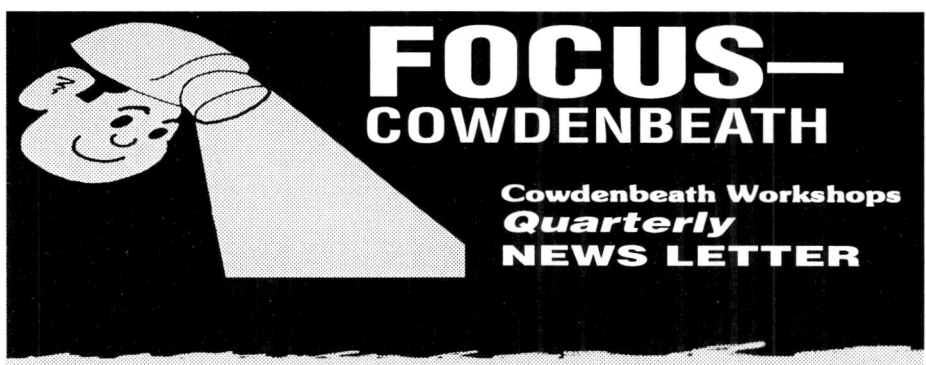

THE 'FUCUS' PLAN - A STRATEGY FOR CLOSURE
CONCOCTED BY IAN MacGREGOR AND CARRIED OUT BY T. MARTIN

THE 'FUCUS' PLAN WAS AS FOLLOWS:-

1. After the strike get rid of the most experienced men.
2. Appoint incompetent Foreman, preferably Scabs, and Green management. Be sure to pick 'YES-MEN' ONLY.
3. Don't recruit Apprentices - and run down manpower.
4. Give away your work to your pals in Private Enterprise.
5. Don't talk to Union Officials.
6. Treat men like dirt. - Lay in the boot till they're Sick.
7. Even if men do a good job and help out Pits in difficulty, totally ignore it.
8. Keep telling the workers they're Skivers and Useless.
9. Whenever things seem to be improving, produce another issue of your Works Magazine to spread gloom and despair.
10. If you get this mix right - men become demoralised, stop trying, and apply for Redundancy.
11. When you get a flood of redundancy applications, you know you have succeeded. You can then blame the men for wanting to close the place.

These are the steps in the 'FUCUS PLAN', the method used to close a factory and then blame it on the Workers.

VERY CLEVER IF IT WORKS AND THE COAL BOARD WILL REWARD THE MANAGER WITH A BIG REDUNDANCY PAYMENT AND A FAT PENSION FOR LIFE!

But:-

WORKERS SHOULD UNDERSTAND EXACTLY WHAT'S GOING ON AT COWDENBEATH.

DON'T BE CONNED BY 'FOCUS' - IT'S ONLY PART OF THE FUCUS PLAN.

IT'S BAD MANAGEMENT, NOT BAD WORKERS, THAT SHUTS FACTORIES.

AND COWDENBEATH MUST HAVE ABOUT THE WORST.

BUT TOO MUCH WAS SACRIFICED FOR TOO LONG, TO FALL FOR THIS DIRTY BUSINESS.

SO DON'T LET THE BASTARDS GRIND YOU DOWN - YOUR DAY WILL COME.

AND THEN THE BOOT WILL BE ON THE OTHER FOOT AND THEY'LL BE GUTTED OUT!

****

Issued by C.D.C.W.

THE END AND AFTERWARDS

Despite the Coal Board denials, the process of closing Cowdenbeath Workshops proceeded, and redundancy followed redundancy. My turn for the 'bullet' came in January 1987 when I was handed my 'voluntary redundancy' with no option.

A campaign continued for some time as a declining labour forced sought guarantees about the long-term future of the Workshops, with the Coal Board denying any plans for closure. But after much speculation, on 13th October 1988, the announcement that Cowdenbeath Workshops, established in 1925, with a record of engineering excellence, was finally to close. The remaining workers were offered redundancy or transfer to Workshops in England. Most took redundancy, but a number gave the transfer option a trial, though few finally settled down South.

Two months later the factory gates were shut except to the buyers and scrap merchants looking for a bargain amongst the machinery and equipment for sale. And so at Christmas 1988, the last link that Cowdenbeath – a town which once boasted 11 pits within it's boundaries - had with the Coal Industry was severed. - Chicago had finally tumbled! ...

CHICAGO TUMBLES

CHAPTER 13

WAS IT WORTHWHILE?

When the Strike was over, and people returned to work without a settlement it was a time for reflection and analysis over the events and the outcome. Thousands of miners had been arrested, hundreds had been sacked and victimised, the Union was split, there were bitter divisions between Strikers and Scabs, family savings had disappeared, debts had been run up and at the end of the day the Coal Board were able to proceed with their massive closure programme.

Was it all worthwhile?

Over the year after the Strike I posed that question to a range of the people who had been actively involved . These are the answers as they gave them at the time.

"I have no regrets about my personal commitment and contribution. If the same situation arose again, I would do it all again I was proud to be part of it"

Bryan Easton

"It had to be done. We were fighting for jobs. The Government engineered the Strike and pre-planned their strategy - but we had no option and I have no regrets. I learnt lessons and I would like to have another go"

David Connor

"When you go into a struggle you cannot be sure you will win. But if you don't struggle you are guaranteed to lose"

Willie Clarke

"She (Mrs Thatcher) just wouldn't give in. But it brought our family closer and I gained some marvellous friends. I'd go through it all again"

Charlotte Lindsay

"The Strike made me a lot of good loyal friends. It could have changed the country for the good"

Gordon Wilson

"If you asked me in terms of what we gained the answer must be no. But in personal terms, before the Strike I hardly knew anyone in Cowdenbeath, and we gained friends we never had before, and for me even that made it worthwhile"

Betty Hynd

"It built Community spirit, and it was a training ground for active members of the NUM for the future"

Brian Russell

"Before the Strike I doubted my own ability to organise and do things but the experience gave me a lot more personal confidence. I'd do it all again if the need arose"

Doreen Meldrum

"The Government were shoving a lot of workers about and we showed that the miners would only allow it up to a point. If only the TUC had backed us the way the CBI back the Coal Board"

Jimmy Whyte (Sacked)

"We were right to go on Strike. It is always worth it to fight for what you believe. No doubt I would do it again"

Harry Robertson

"Whether the Strike was the right course of action at the time or not I wasn't sure, but for once in my life I felt I was fighting for something better, not for just myself but people like me. To have at least experienced that feeling, if only once in a lifetime, makes me conclude that I'm glad I was part of it"

Gordon Maxwell

"I was glad it was over, but it brought people together. If it was to happen again I would do the same"

Lorna Lindsay

"Yes, it was worth it. It was absolutely brilliant - well worth the fight"

Lorraine Adams

WAS IT WORTHWHILE?

"We had to have a go - look back now and see what's happening to the Coal Industry despite what they told us at the time"

George Selkirk

"It was one of the best years of my life. Then to be chosen as 1985 Citizen of the Year in Cowdenbeath was fantastic. I was very proud and I have no regrets"

Helen Thomson

"There was really no alternative - Yes the Strike was worthwhile"

Eddie Garvie

"I never firmly believed we could win against the Government. The victory lay in the Community involvement and I was glad to experience and be part of that"

Cathie Cunningham

"We had to fight. I have no regrets and I'd do it all again if I could"

Ronnie Campbell (Victimised)

"I would not wish what we suffered on anyone - but - I would not have missed the experience for anything, in terms of how people came together in the sense of community"

Jack Allan

These views are representative of the large number of people who played some active part in the Strike, and they remained virtually the same years after.

In spite of Arthur Scargill's absurd statement at the end of the Strike that *'The Coal Board have won nothing'*, none of the people in the front line at Cowdenbeath claimed that the outcome was in any way a victory. Of course neither did people in the leadership use the word 'defeat' because too many mining families had sacrificed so much for so long to be made feel it had been in vain.

Nevertheless, with the benefit of what Mick McGahey often describes as *'the most exact science of all-hindsight'* it can no longer be denied that the Strike totally failed to accomplish it's aims and the consequences of that failure have been tragic for the miners. But, as the previous comments from those who were involved show, there were very positive features which made it worthwhile for them. The solidarity of the strikers themselves, the massive support internationally, nationally and within their own area, to sustain them morally and financially. The emergence of the women both as individuals and as a collective group, without whom the Strike could not have continued for so long.

Bonds within and between families were strengthened. Working people who hardly knew each other, both here and throughout the country became brothers and sisters in a common cause on marches, in rallies and on the picket line. Young men and woman matured in the struggle, discovering talents and resources within themselves they never imagined. Whilst the Strike did not achieve it's objectives, it was invaluable in terms of personal development and community spirit.

ANALYSING THE OUTCOME

As Mrs Thatcher has confirmed in her memoirs, the aim of the Government, planned long in advance, was to inflict a crippling blow to the Miners Union, and to issue a warning message to any other section of British workers who were tempted to challenge her policies. In this she succeeded.

As most commentators and active participants now acknowledge, although to their credit the Scottish Miners Officials had already recognised it in the early stages of the Strike, there were serious weaknesses in the strategy adopted by Scargill and the national leadership. Indeed it could be argued with justification that the NUM did not have a strategy at all for winning the Strike, as I amongst many others in Scotland suggested in the early days.

This was in sharp contrast to the Government who had carefully prepared for the Strike well in advance, and during it's course were plotting and planning along with the Coal Board day and night throughout it's entire course. By comparison it was clear that the NUM leadership was not sitting day in and day out discussing the dispute, every aspect of the dispute, the strategy and tactics of the dispute.

There were serious mistakes which made a victory virtually impossible, and certainly the Cowdenbeath leadership accepted that in their analysis of the Strike. At the start there should have been a ballot. This was always a weakness. It divided the Union members, it was a powerful propaganda weapon for the Government in the battle for public opinion, and it allowed leaders of unions who could have taken crucial industrial action (eg the Powerworkers) the excuse not to, on the grounds that if the miners can't win a strike call among their own members, they couldn't expect other workers to put their jobs on the line.

Whether a ballot before the Strike could have been won is doubtful, but there is an overwhelming view that a ballot would have been successful in April, May or June, and should have been risked.

Mass picketing was also a major tactical error. It was totally counterproductive - in relation to just about everything - but certainly in relation to Nottingham. Perhaps if the leadership had concentrated in Nottingham on mass meetings and demonstrations at the beginning rather than mass picketing and then gone for a National Ballot, we would have had all Britain's miners on Strike. That of course would not have guaranteed a victory over the Government but it would have massively strengthened the Union in the campaign for solidarity action and public support.

Throughout the Strike not only was mass picketing unsuccessful in preventing the flow of coal or the return of 'scabs' it presented the miners to the British Public, courtesy of biased television, as a mob bent on picket line violence. Yet despite all the evidence to the contrary Scargill was still calling for mass pickets up to four weeks from the end of the Strike, a strategy which had patently failed.

As it was, both the decision not to ballot, and the mass picketing, with the attendant violence, also affected 'Her Majesty's Loyal Opposition' in Parliament - the Labour Party - whose leadership backed away from giving full support to the miners, despite good conference decisions. Time and again Thatcher taunted Kinnock in the House of Commons over *'his silence'* over what was going on in the Strike, and he was unable to respond effectively, acting indeed as though the miners were an embarrassment to the Party.

If any one lesson was to be learned from the miners strike it was that in modern times the industrial muscle of a single union alone cannot win a dispute with the Government. The miners strike was not just a industrial struggle, it was also a political struggle. In that circumstance, the concentration should have been on using every possible opportunity and means to argue the case for coal as against the Governments strategy, and to put this case before millions of British people.

There was a viable case for coal, and what was needed was to develop a national campaign to win public opinion, exposing the weakness of the Government's energy policy. Instead of that the mass picketing diverted the public's attention from the real issues, and made the argument one about violence and the right of individuals to go to work.

I suspect that at the time despite the material support given by many people to relieve the hardship of miners families, they would have found it difficult to explain just what the miners case was. A lot of people thought the miners were just trying to defend the past, an historically dated fuel, against a future of nuclear power and other sources of energy. There was a future for coal, but the argument was not presented to the British public as it should have been.

Certainly in Scotland the Union led by Mick McGahey were more conscious of the need to win support among the people, and cultivated alliances with an array of Scottish industrial, political, social and religious bodies, to exert pressure on the Government.

It is to the credit of the Cowdenbeath Strike Centre leadership that they identified the importance of this strategy from the start. Despite some initial opposition in the Committee, an almost unique feature of their activities were the weekly meetings which were open not just to the Strikers but to their families and the general public.

Speakers came from other trade unions - seamen, dockers, railwaymen, local government, teachers, from local factories and workplaces, ministers and priests, social workers and rights officers, MP's, and the MEP, councillors, representative from the SNP, the Labour and Communist Parties in political forums and of course the Scottish officials.

Not only did this boost the morale of the Strikers but it reached out to their wives and family and the general public, so that they were aware of what was happening but also that they understood the case for coal and the politics of it all. It was a model for others to emulate in developing broad support in the community, but sadly it was not the pattern throughout the coalfields.

IF ONLY - - -

When looking back on the Strike there are the inevitable 'If Only's'. 'If Only' the dockers had stayed on Strike. 'If Only' the power workers had gone out on Strike. 'If Only' NACODS hadn't sold out. 'If Only' the TUC and the Labour Party had really mobilised support throughout the country. 'If Only' Nottingham had come out with us.

With the benefit of having read MacGregor's book *'The Enemies Within'* it is clear that he recognised the crucial importance of the Nottingham miners, and was convinced that *'if we could keep this vast and prosperous coalfield going, however long it took, we would succeed'*

However, it is clear that most of the 'If Only's' were very unlikely in Thatcher's Britain in 1984, because of the relative affluence of some sections of workers and the impact of the Tory philosophy of *'mind thyself'* individualism, which undermines solidarity action, alongside the legitimate fear of unemployment amongst many other workers. Other ' Only's' were in fact rendered impossible by the strategy employed by the NUM leadership under Scargill, as outlined previously.

All of that of course is now speculation and we will never know whether even if some of the 'If Only's' had been achieved, the miners would have emerged with a measure of victory. It is apparent now that total victory was never possible, once Nottingham was a lost cause early in the Strike. However, if victory was not a realistic goal at least there were possibilities of a compromise which would have kept the Union in tact and *'live to fight another day'*.

The July talks offered such a possibility. If Macgregor is to be believed, McGahey and he were *'getting closer together'* at their discussions in Edinburgh on 8th June and he claims that Jimmy Cowan (MacGregor's Deputy) said to him *'I think the Communist Party is ready to settle'*. However MacGregor replied *'I think McGahey is - but not Scargill'*. Finally in the July talks Scargill rejected the deal, apparently still believing a decisive victory was possible.

Interestingly Margaret Thatcher reveals in her recent memoirs that there were two occasions she was worried about the outcome of the Strike. The first was when the dockers were on Strike, whilst these 'July Talks' were in progress, in which she felt the Coal Board were giving too much away. She says she was *'enormously relieved'* when the negotiations collapsed and the dock strike ended two days later.

The second occasion was when NACODS took a Strike decision on 26th September. This was the time she *'felt most concern'* faced with NACODS decision and the uncertainty of what solidarity support might follow from the resolution of support at the TUC Conference earlier in the month. MacGregor claims he had to calm her nerves at the time, but in the event neither of the two dangers materialised. NACODS settled and the TUC proved impotent. Nevertheless the NACODS agreement provided an opportunity to snatch a modest victory from a deteriorating situation, but Scargill rejected the possibility of compromise. Later in January 1985, McGahey was known to favour a compromise based on the NACODS October formula, and an acceptance of **some** closures, but nothing came of that either.

What might have been is course now conjecture, and we will never know for certain if a deal could have been secured which would have changed the direction or pace of Government policy. However what is clear is that the miners ultimately paid a terrible price for the failure to reach a settlement. The final result indeed did not leave them even the opportunity to *'fight another day'* which an earlier compromise would have made possible.

The outcome of the Miners Strike was a decisive victory for the Government and a personal triumph for Mrs Thatcher. Having been rescued from pending political disaster by the Falklands War, where she defeated the enemy without she had now defeated the *'enemy within'* the miners, and if she could beat the miners, who could possibly stand in her way? And for the Trade Union Movement, it was clearly a time for reflection and new ideas.

SOLID TO THE END.

In Fife 90% of the mining Labour force were still on Strike when the Strike finally ended. In Cowdenbeath Workshops the figure was 85%, but the majority of those who were at work were people who lived outside Cowdenbeath and indeed not in any mining community at all.

Of the men and women who lived in the area covered by the

WAS IT WORTHWHILE?

Cowdenbeath Strike Centre 95% remained out, a remarkable figure given all that the miners and their families had endured. There were a number of reasons for this. As outlined in a previous chapter there was the underlying historical militant tradition, of the Fife miners, and the specific political features of Cowdenbeath.

In a town whose very existence was because of coal, and where almost everyone had some connection at present or in the past with the Coal Industry, it was just not acceptable to 'scab'. It meant becoming an outcast in the community, the one thing you would be remembered for in days to come. And to be honest for some there was an element of fear and intimidation which operarted as well. I have no doubt there were a few who would like to have gone back but were deterred. I also have no doubt that afterwards to a man (or woman) they were thankful and relieved that they did not, and were able to hold their heads up high with their workmates when it was all over.

But the role of those who gave leadership - the Strike Committee, in alleviating the hardship and maintaining the morale of the Strikers and their families, and extending the campaign into the community should not be underestimated. Whatever the failings of the national leadership in pursuing the objective of the Strike, the Cowdenbeath leadership conducted the local scene, in a responsible manner, with clarity of purpose and efficiency of operation.

When I asked Eddie Garvie after the Strike to identify what he thought was a highlight of the Strike or their greatest achievement, he responded in these terms. *"In twelve months of struggle there were of course many highlights, memorable events and incidents which will remain with me forever, but no doubt the most remarkable fact was that we held together all that time.*
If you had asked me before the Strike if men and women would be prepared to endure a year on Strike to try and defend their jobs, and their communities, I would have had the gravest doubts .. and yet - they did - and that must be the greatest achievement of all".

CHAPTER 14

TEN YEARS AFTER – PERSONAL REFLECTIONS

Looking back ten years later, when it is much easier to evaluate the Strike and its consequences, it still seems like a nightmare. All those terrible events which happened during that twelve months now hardly seems believable and yet they happened. No doubt it was the most bitter industrial conflict in British history, between miners fighting purely to defend their jobs and their communities, and a Government hellbent on inflicting a massive defeat on the Miners Union as a prelude to an all round attack on the Union Movement and the living standards of working people.

In her book 'The Downing Street Years', Margaret Thatcher spells it out *'the coal strike was always about far more than uneconomic pits. It was a political strike and so it's out come had a significance far beyond the economic sphere'*

Most commentators agree that there were points in the Strike when a settlement could have been reached, albeit not on terms that the miners would have accepted at the beginning. But recognising the determination of the Government, and the weaknesses of their own position - a divided workforce and the inability of the TUC and other unions to deliver solidarity action - the Union could have emerged with a degree of dignity and creditability, to carry on the political campaign for Coal.

On one hand the Government had those wider political aims which required a total victory, and tragically Scargill too saw the miners strike as a political struggle against the Tories with his men as the shocktroops of the Labour movement. So compromise between the Coal Board and the Unions was prevented by Government interference and Scargill's intrangience. It was a fight to the finish - all or nothing. In retrospect Thatcher must have welcomed Scargill as a blessing in disguise.

In the years which followed, not just the miners, but the whole trade union movement and millions of British people have suffered the consequences of defeat. Thatcher fought and won two further elections. She sold off the 'family silver' privatising Gas, Electricity and British Telecom, undermined the Health Service, Education, Housing and Social Welfare provision, and presided over mass unemployment and widespread despair in British Society, widening the gap between rich and poor to a degree never seen before and creating an almost permanent 'underclass' devoid of hope about the future.

Trade union membership has plunged from 12 million to about 7 1/2 million, as Britain's manufacturing base has shrunk, unemployment reached new heights, and many workers are employed in part-time or temporary jobs. A series of anti-trade union laws have severely weakened the ability of trade unions to take action in defence of their jobs, wages and working conditions, and British workers now have less employment rights than most of their European counterparts. Even the Wages Councils which guaranteed minimum wage rates in service industries have been abolished.

How much of all this would have happened if somehow the miners could have emerged victorious can only be speculation, but no doubt the trade union movement and the British people have paid a heavy price for their defeat.

Ian MacGregor, his job done, is now long gone and eventually of course too Thatcher was deposed as she became an increasing liability to the Tories, especially with the sinking of her Poll Tax 'flag-ship' to be replaced just in time by 'nice' Mr Major to win the Tories another General Election against an inept Labour opposition - but the policies remain.

As for the coal industry there has been a continual contraction, as colliery after colliery has been closed, with certainly up till 1992 little opposition from the miners who worked there. In the aftermath of the Strike, such was the bitterness, the despair and indeed the debts among the miners, that a vote at any colliery in Scotland would have resulted in a vote of closure. Understandably there was little rank and file opposition to that process so that today Scotland had but one British Coal Colliery at Castlebridge feeding Longannet Power Station, with Frances Colliery at Kirkcaldy kept only on a 'care and maintenance' basis.

A Workers Co-operative was established in 1992 at Monktonhall in the Lothians with miners chipping in some £10,000 a piece. In the view of the NUM Scottish leadership, and shared by myself, this was a risky venture from the start. The costs of equipping and maintaining a modern colliery run into tens of millions of pounds, but Monktonhall was re-opened on a shoestring budget and the co-operative concept seems doomed and the men's investment in jeopardy.

It has to be acknowledged of course that the mining industry has been in almost continuous decline for around seventy years. In 1923 at it's peak 1,250,000 men had produced 300 million tons of coal. By Nationalisation 700,000 men were producing 200 million tons of coal. By the early '80's after massive investment 200,000 men were producing 100 million tons. New sources of energy, North Sea gas, oil and nuclear power have all cut inroads into the monopoly that coal once had.

Since the Strike that pattern of closure has accelerated, and in the whole of Britain the number of collieries declined from 176 employing 180,000 men in 1984 to 50 employing 40,000 men in October 1992, a scale of closure exceeding even that forecast by Arthur Scargill before the 1984 Strike. It must be small consolation for him to be proved right. And even those men who are left are divided between two unions, the NUM and the UDM, formed in Nottingham during the Strike, a breach that no serious attempt has been made to heal, despite their common interest in preserving jobs.

But even the 50 pits still surviving in 1992 were not safe. The run down of the Coal Industry was to continue and in October 1992 British Coal announced that 31 more pits would be due for closure as the demand for coal was projected to fall to around 40 million tones, the result of a massive switch to power generation by gas by the privatised electricity companies.

The reaction throughout the country was unbelievable, since to that time, there had been little opposition to pit closures, and indeed the preceding year 21,000 jobs had gone from the industry, almost un-noticed. A storm of protest from every quarter of British society shook the Government. The Miners Union organised a lobby of Parliament and a mass demonstration in London against the pit closures on Wednesday 19 October, followed by another Mass demonstration on the Sunday, involving some 240,000 people.

London had seen nothing like it since the war. It was as if the announcement of pit closures was the last straw for a British public, sick of Government policies which had caused de-industrialisation, cuts in public services, mass unemployment and growing poverty and homelessness.

They came from every part of Britain, from the stricken Welsh valleys and the gutted shipbuilding communities of Tyneside, from the pit villages of Durham, Yorkshire and Nottingham, from the closure threatened hospitals of the capital, even from the stockbroker belt of Surrey, And they came to say *'Enough is enough'*!

My wife Mary and I travelled to London for the March and Lobby from Coventry, where we were on holiday, on a miners bus from the closed Kersley Colliery. I have been on many marches in my life but none could match that day as over 100,00 people marched from Hyde Park through Kensington. Every building we passed had people at windows cheering us on, big penthouses had banners hanging from them and the streets resounded to the cries of support. Arthur Scargill the much reviled villain of the 1984-85 Strike, the man they loved to hate, was a hero on this day and I saw him presented with flowers on the march by people who nine years before would have jeered and booed at the sight of him.

The demonstration ended back in Hyde Park where the huge gathering cheered speaker after speaker from the ranks of MP's and trade union leaders as they condemned the Government and expressed support for the miners.

The public backlash, it's ferocity matched only by it's unexpectedness, shook the Government to the core. Even it's own backbenchers were up in arms, especially those who had collieries in their constituencies, and the Industry Minister Hesseltine was forced to retreat - a humiliating climbdown. A review of those pits under threat was promised and for the moment the closure programme was halted.

TEN YEARS AFTER – PERSONAL REFLECTIONS

In an endeavour to keep the pressure on the Government, the Scottish Area of the NUM organised a National March from Glasgow to London along a route which would cover 630 miles and go through the coalfield areas. Six miners led by George Bolton, the Scottish President, were to undertake the ordeal, but it was decided that it should be preceded with a short march through the Fife Coalfield.

On November 13th 1992 the walkers gathered at Lochore Miners Institute and were accompanied by District Councillors John Simpson, Joe Paterson, Allan Gray and myself, along with Community Councillors and former miners, on the journey through Lochgelly, gathering money from many well-wishers en route to a Civic reception in the Cowdenbeath Bowling Club, where Provost Margaret Millar and other councillors wished them well on their long trail. In the event the March lasted five weeks and Bolton and his team were well received as they passed down through England to arrive in London on 19th December to a reception from the TUC.

The march brought a great deal of publicity for the Miners campaign, but despite that kind of pressure and the assurance of an honest review of the closure programme, once again the Government reneged on it's promises, and played for time, letting the fury subside, only to come back twelve months later to a situation that a number of pits had gone, thousands of men taken redundancy and less than 20 pits were said to be required to meet the country's needs, although by this time Coal was actually being imported to fuel certain Power stations. In that year the initial fury had been assuaged and at the time of writing the prospect is that soon only some 15 pits will be left in the country.

The systematic dismantling of the coal industry in Britain, was set in motion in 1984 and brought about the miners strike. The resulting miners defeat in that Strike was the signal for full steam ahead for the Government, and the cost has been massive pit closures and the loss of thousands of jobs which have never been replaced.

It seems to me that this pattern will continue and there will be few pits left to privatise in Britain in 1994. Certainly nuclear power which was seen to be the great threat to the coal industry is now in disrepute but the latest estimates of massive oil and gas reserves in the waters around Britain, along with the new technological developments which make them attainable, point to gas being the main source of energy for electrical power generation for decades to come.

In fact the newly created Power Generation bodies have a foot in both camps and the piping of gas direct from the North Sea into the power stations is already a reality, and will continue, now that the control of our sources of energy and power supply have been handed over to the giant monopolies who dominate our economy. Coal's place in that economy seems destined for almost oblivion, as it is inconceivable that the collieries which have been closed could ever be re-opened.

Of course it could be argued, and has been for many years, that men should not have to descend to the bowels of the earth, to risk life and limb in hazardous conditions, and to suffer the dreaded lung diseases caused by dust inhalation, costing many lives before their natural span.

Indeed few miners ever wanted their sons to go down the pit, but there was little option in mining villages in the past. Perhaps we should be glad the pits are closed and that these lives are not lost or our countryside despoiled by the ravages of mining. We no longer live in the shadow of the pit bing and for that we should be thankful.

But there is a greater shadow over us. It is the shadow of mass unemployment, which demoralises millions of our people, leaving them without hope and purpose. And we have witnessed the destruction of mining towns and villages, and a way of community life which had many positive features that have not been replaced.

Whilst mining was a dangerous and difficult occupation, and it could be seen perhaps as a blessing that it has virtually disappeared - that has to be set against the alternative for thousands of people which is even worse. The slogan of the 1984-85 Miners Strike - **COAL NOT DOLE** - has been totally vindicated by events since those tumultuous times ten years ago.

AND WHAT OF COWDENBEATH?

The closure of the Central Workshops in December 1988 finally ended Cowdenbeath's connection with the coal industry after 138 years. That industry had shaped every feature of life in the town, economic, social cultural, sporting and political, and when it ended there was a knock-on effect. The town declined, unemployment reaching 15% officially and much more in reality. The Workshops site is now an Industrial Estate, but the group of small firms there employ but a fraction of the 600 people who entered those gates every morning twenty years ago.

Former miners in their fifties never worked again when they got their redundancy cheques, the others who got their living from coal are dispersed all over the place, and young people hang around the streets of Cowdenbeath with little to do and not much hope of finding a job.

The High Street is sprinkled with closed businesses and charity shops. The last working men's clubs have gone, and even the Miners Welfare Institute, the former Strike Centre, is now a struggling Night Club. The local Public Band once financed by the subscriptions from the miners, barely survives on Council grants. Cowdenbeath F.C. now attracts only a couple of hundred loyal supporters, and depends on Stock Car Racing to keep the gates open.

With European money and Council grants, efforts have been made to renovate and clean up buildings on the High Street and to improve the environment, with some success. Reminders of the former coal industry are few. A Swimming Pool now stands at the site of the old Cowdenbeath No.7 Pit, (to be joined by a new Sports Centre). Soon youngsters who play on the Dora Golf Course, may well wonder at the 'pit tub' at the entry and puzzle at the names of the holes - Lumphinnans, Peewit, Kirkford, Little Raith, Fordell, Moss-beath, Cowdenbeath, Mossmorran, Foulford.

Older people will tell them that these were the names of local pits. Interestingly, when the other nine holes come along as promised, there will still be enough pits names left to go with them as well, as Cowdenbeath once was the centre of a coalfield with more pits than will exist in the whole of Britain in 1994.

Just as the demise of the coal industry affected many former features of the life in Cowdenbeath, so it has had it's impact on the politics of the town. As outlined at the beginning of the book, the town had a remarkable political history and consistently elected Communist councillors from 1935 till 1974, such as 'Old Bob' Selkirk, given the Freedom of the Burgh, and Willie Sharp, the last Provost of the town, and the first Communist

Provost in Britain. Whilst the townspeople themselves may have though little about it, this made Cowdenbeath something of a novelty in Britain.

Also as explained earlier there were many outstanding Communist Miners leaders who came from this area, and went on to the leading positions in the Scottish Area - and traditionally Communist influence was strong in the Central Fife pits, continuing up to the 1984 Strike. In Cowdenbeath at that time, the composition of the Strike Committee itself reflected that Communist presence, and embraced a number of young men who were already involved and were being prepared for union leadership in the future.

The reverse in the Strike, followed by demoralisation, redundancies and eventual closures in the Fife mining industry, including Cowdenbeath Workshops, destroyed that traditional Communist base, and dispersed those who had been developing as it's next generation of active members. Added to that the collapse in the '80's of the Soviet Union and the Eastern European Countries, shattered the illusions of many members and finally led to the dissolution of the British Communist Party.

For the first time in seventy years there is no Communist Party Branch in Cowdenbeath, and perhaps symbolically it's former premises in Victoria Buildings on High Street now stands charred and in ruins, the victim of a fire. When I pass there I look back nostalgically on the countless meetings we held there discussing debating and solving the problems of the world, when we still believed that life held something better for working people than they experienced in our country. Such hopes and dreams have been weakened in the harsh light of reality.

For many of us the events of recent years have been difficult to come to terms with; indeed the experience has been for some people akin to that of a minister who wakes up one day to realise there is no God!

However life goes on, and whatever happened elsewhere in the world or how wrong we might have been about what was going on there, we cannot erase the tremendous work done in Cowdenbeath and elsewhere in Fife by Communists over many years in the interests or ordinary people, a record that is acknowledged in the community. It is no accident that at the last Council elections I was returned as a District Councillor, standing as a Democratic Left candidate - an organisation which arose out of the former

Communist Party, attempting to carry on all that was best in its local tradition.

Indeed commenting on the results of the 1992 District Elections the authoritative magazine 'Scottish Affairs' (No.2 Winter 1992) said *'Perhaps the most remarkable ward result in Scotland was the one in Dunfermline South East in which a candidate of the 'Democratic Left' - the successor of the British Communist Party - took a seat from Labour. Given all that has happened in the world, he must have been a very remarkable candidate'.*

It is a unique situation in Britain, but then Cowdenbeath has always been something special in the British political map. Despite the praise of the authors of the article, however, what was remarkable was not the candidate, but those who for many years before and after I arrived on the scene gave so much to the people of the town and earned their confidence and respect.

They too were part of the mining fabric of Cowdenbeath, now consigned to the history books.

WHERE ARE THEY NOW?

And what of the local leaders of the Strike, those who undertook the mammoth task of heading the strikers for that momentous year. Brian Russell, the Chairman - now a bus-driver, Bryan Easton, the Secretary - a factory worker, Jack Allan and Eddie Garvie took redundancy and retired from paid working life, though Jack is still active in community affairs, and both hold positions in the local Retired Mineworkers Branch.

John Simpson remained in the Workshops till closure, but became a Labour Councillor again and now leads the administration on Dunfermline District Council. Iain Chalmers still works at the threatened Frances Pit, but after the Strike developed a successful sideline in miners memorabilia, such as Colliery Commemoration plates. Willie Muir is at Castlebridge Colliery, Jim Hardie works for the District Council, Harry Robertson is employed at Edinburgh Air Port, Rab Ross is on the oil rigs, Frank Kirby works as an electrician in various locations. Gordon Wilson became a taxi-driver and Harry Cunningham returned to college and is now a lecturer.

Of the men they led, there are now less than thirty from this area working in the mining industry. In the wake of the Strike there were huge redundancies, and many men left with sizable redundancy payments. After paying off accumulated debts, some bought their houses with the cash, or a new car or took a holiday. A few overwhelmed with having so much money at one time 'unloaded' it to the publicans and betting shops or spent like millionaires for a very short time till they were broke. Others bought taxis and plied for hire; one or two invested in ill-fated businesses.

Many were persuaded by 'financial consultants' to put their money into stock and bonds - sometimes to their regret. Indeed one of the funnier things I came across a few years ago was in the Dunfermline Library where I witnessed the hitherto unusual sight of ex-miners waiting their turn to read the Financial Times! Most of the older men never worked again, whilst the younger ones are scattered all over the place, often in jobs of lesser status.

My own family example was that my son Harry emigrated to Gibraltar to find work, Gordon is employed as a mechanical Technician on the oil-rigs where he comes across numerous ex-Coal Board employees, and Neil retrained as a bricklayer.

They, like many of the former workshops men I meet nowadays, however, still miss the comradeship and community spirit of the coal industry, and when they meet over a pint, the stories of work and the Strike go on long into the evening. Fortunately they can now look back on those dramatic days and laugh at some of the lighter moments, even indeed with a degree of nostalgia.

As for the Women Support Group, the officials Lorraine Adams, Heather Wilson and Doreen Meldrum have now got families of their own. Helen Thomson left the area and has a shop in Newburgh, Cathie Cunningham is a Community Worker, and the others have, after all that activity, more or less gone back to being housewives and mothers, although Sandra Taylor has become Chairperson of Cowdenbeath Community Council.

During the Strike many of these women were politicised. They did things they never dreamed of before, discovering strengths within themselves they never realised and gained in personal confidence and assertiveness. Near the end when the Labour Party were making a very determined bid to recruit new members from within the Strike Centres, some of them joined. Also attempts were made to keep the womens groups in existence, but both these moves to keep them active eventually failed, and the reality is that the women in the main returned fairly soon to the lives they knew before the Strike.

Certainly they had gone through an unforgettable experience, but whilst they cannot but be much more aware of the realities of life in Britain today, there is little outward evidence that it had a lasting effect on their activities. Perhaps it would have been different if they had not seen their efforts end finally in defeat - but who knows?

At the end of the Strike, Lorraine Adams said *'I have no regrets. For a year I ate, slept and breathed the Strike. we showed that miners would stand up and fight for their rights, and at the end we gave in graciously, and if another Strike took place, I would be back with the Soup Pot!'* But sadly (or maybe gladly) her soup pot will never be needed again to feed miners and their families on Strike.

The 1984/85 National Miners Strike will go down in British history as the last great miners strike ever to take place after almost 150 years of conflict within that industry. It's outcome settled not just the fate of the coal industry, but led to Thatcher's transformation of the whole political scene, with devastating effect on millions of the British working class.

Those loyal miners and their families who gave their all, even if they did not all know it then, were not just fighting for their pits and communities, they were the front line troops defending all of us from the perils of Thatcherism. When they fell, the road was open and we are still suffering the consequences, ten year later.

The men and women of Cowdenbeath were part of that terrible, yet glorious battle. They gave more in that struggle than can reasonably be expected by the rest of us from any group of people carrying the banner on our behalf, and no doubt many of Thatcher's later victims in other industries and occupations will wish they had done more to help them at the time. The miners and their families are entitled to look back now with pride, and we with humility, at their achievement and I hope future generations will also be proud to find the names of their family in this record of the Strike and the Roll of Honour it contains.

1984-85 MINERS STRIKE
ROLL OF HONOUR

**PEOPLE IN AREA COVERED BY COWDENBEATH STRIKE CENTRE
WHO REMAINED ON STRIKE OVER THE ENTIRE YEAR**

Employed in Cowdenbeath Workshops and Resident in Cowdenbeath.

R. Adie	M. Jarrett	A. Nicol
A. Aitken	D. Hynd	A. Park
R. Aitchison	J. Hynd	A. Paterson
W. Aitchison	W. Hodge	Mrs J. Paterson
J. Allan	J. Hutchison	T. Peden
Mrs M. Allan	Mrs J. Hodge	A. Peters
W. Allan	A. Jones	A. Philip
A. Arthur	A. Johnstone	W. Philip
W. Arthur	T. Kinnell	C. Reekie
C. Baird	C. Kelly	R. Reid
J. Bartie	G. Kent	Mrs H Reilly
D. Bauld	J. Kelligan	H. Robertson
C. Black	R. Kinnell	A. Ross
J. Black	F. Kirby	J. Ross
J. Bowman	J. Kirkpatrick	R. Ross
C. Brooks	T. King	B. Russell
J. Carr	A. Lees	C. Russell
R. Clark	W. Lees	G. Russell
D. Connor	A. Lindsay	G. Selkirk
C. Copeland	L. Linton	W. Selfridge
J. Cowan	J. Lockhart	J. Simpson
H. Crombie	W. Lynch	R. Simpson
H. Cunningham	A. Lumsden	A. Scott
T. Cunningham	M. McKee	W. Small
Mrs S. Dickson	A. Mackie	G. Smith
R. Donaldson	T. McDonald	R. Smith
J. Dryburgh	I. McIntyre	F. Somerville
R. Dryburgh	G. McKenzie	J. Speirs
B. Easton	A. Mc Kinlay	A. Stanley
M. Easton	D. McLean	N. Stark
N. Forsyth	K. McLuckie	N. Thomson
S. Fowler	G. McQueen	W. Thomson
J. Fowler	J. Mair	B. Walker
E. Gibb	W. Malcolm	A. Warrander
R. Gibson	A. Marshall	S. Watson
Mrs J. Gordon	W. Marshall	C. Weir
I. Gillard	G. Maxwell	A. Whitelaw
D. Gordon	H. Maxwell	D. Whitelaw
P. Graham	N. Maxwell	I. Wilkie
A. Haddow	G. Menzies	A. Wilson
J. Hardie Snr.	D. Miller	R. Wilson
W. Harrison	W. Mitchell	W. Wilson
J. Hardie Jnr.	J. Moffat	W. Winsborough
J. Harrower	J. Muir	D. Whyte
J. Heron	J. Muirhead	J. Whyte
A. Hood	J. Mullen	W. Wright
D. Hughes	K. Nicol	

Cont

NOTE: These lists are based on Strike Centre records. If anyone has been missed, please accept my apologies. **A.M.**

Employed at Cowdenbeath Workshops but resident elsewhere

HILL OF BEATH
A. Bernard
S. Ferguson
E. McKee
W. Sinclair

LUMPHINNANS
A. Couper
F. Fleming
J. Lowe
J. McCusker
A. Mackie
W. Malcolm
G. Reid
R. Reekie

BURNTISLAND
M. White
W. Booth

PERTH
B. Reilly

FREUCHIE
J. Philip

CROSSGATES
R. Crichton

KELTY
G. Adger
T. Dickson
A. Elliot
W. Easterbrook
R. Graham
G. Hatton
G. Hepburn
W. Hunter
T. Logan
A. Lowe
A. McHale
D. Menzies
H. Miller
A. Paterson
J. Semple
J. Small
D. Wardrope

KINGLASSIE
B. Gavin

BALLINGRY
A. Campbell
A. Kilgour
T. King
B. McLinden
C. Paterson
T. Ratcliffe
G. Rowley
A. Shields

CROSSHILL
J. Leighton

LOCHORE
G. Brown
J. Gallacher
G. McDonald
J. Moffat
J. Paterson
J. Ritchie
R. Smith
K. Wilson

CARDENDEN
A. Arnott
T. Bennett
R. Birrell
L. Campbell
W. Duffy
I. Fleming
G. Harley
G. Jack
D. Kinnell
W. Findlay
C. McCrae
D. Morgan
A. Munro
D. Murray
R. Paterson
J. Rattray
J. Ritchie
J. Shand
R. Sharp
D. Shepherd
C. Stevenson
D. Thomson
P. Wallace
J. Walker
J. Ward
J. Walker

LOCHGELLY
J. Beveridge
D. Beveridge
Mrs E. Beveridge
G. Bratchie
A. Brown
R. Campbell
J. Clark
J. Connolly
S. Corrigan
J. Ferris
D. Fyfe
A. Gavin
W. Handyside
G. Hannah
G. Hood
L. Glancy

K. Graham
J. Hamill
H. Hoggan
R. Hunter
W. King
D. Lees
A. Lamond
A. McFadyen
W. McLelland
B. Mathews
P. Murphy
P. Ramsay
R. Reid

DUNFERMLINE
I. Archibald
R. Baxter
J. Campbell
G. Duncan
E. Garvie
J. Nicol
C. Marnoch
C. Tocher
A. Kirk

FALKLAND
G. Brooksband

HALBEATH
W. Bauld
L. Linton

KINROSS
I. Inglis
R. McLaren

COALTOWN OF BALGONIE
D. Kyle

THORNTON
W. Swan

METHILHILL
S. Pratt

INVERKEITHING
J. McGowan

KIRKCALDY
J. Feechan
A. Hamilton
J. Inglis
J. McCord
J. Thomson
H. Wright

GLENROTHES
S. Loney

TULLIBODY
J. Banks

Cont

Resident in Cowdenbeath & District but employed elsewhere in Coal Industry

BOWHILL WASHERY
J. Couper
G. Whisker

COMRIE COLLIERY
R. Aitken
J. Bell
A. Beveridge
J. Brown
W. Campbell
P. Clark
A. Connor
J. O'Donnell
D. Drummond
J. Drummond
G. Duthie
P. Fairley
D. Forbes
W. Forgan – (Lumphinnans)
C. Fraser
J. Gow
A. Harrower
S. Hay
M. Henderson
A. Hunter
A. Hynd
C. Jennings
A. Johnston
J. Johnston
K. Johnstone
A. Law
A. Lawrie
D. Livingstone
S. McAdam
A. McAuley
D. McKay
J. McLeod
P. Meldrum
J. Millar
A. Morgan
W. Maxwell
D. Neilson
J. Neish
I. Paterson
W. Paterson
G. Pye
R. Nicholson
R. Ramage
W. Small
S. Smith
N. Stark
J. Sweeney
J. Thomson
B. Whitelaw
D. Whitelaw
J. Whitelaw
A. Whyte

SEAFIELD COLLIERY
J. Bain
T. Campbell
I. Chalmers
J. Dovey
P. Glancy
B Glencross
J. Haxton
P. Henderson
T. Henderson
I. Johnstone
J. Kaleta Snr.
J. Kaleta Jnr.
J. Jamieson
A. Leishman
C. McCormack
D. McKean
A. Park
J. Pratt
D. Rattray
W. Ritchie
J. Sherry
J. Sneddon
C. Stark
R. Steedman – (Kingseat)
D. Taylor
D. Watson
R. Watson
A. Wotherspoon

FRANCES COLLIERY
W. Allan
A. Baxter
A. Paterson
J. Cook
M. Duffy – Lumph
B. Fairley
A. Fox – Lumph
T. Gilfillan
A. Gray
T. Hoggan
D. Hotchkiss
W. Jones
T. Kay
W. Muir –Lumph
D. Sullivan
R. Watson
R. Wilson – Lumph
A. Wotherspoon
E. Young

CASTLEHILL COLLIERY
R. Beattie
H. Clements
J. Crichton
J. O'Donnell
S. Duthie
H. Easton
D. Gribbin
S. Hutton
K. Hynd
W. Penman
D. Philip – Lumph
A. Smith
B. Stein
F. Stewart
S. Watkins

SOLSGIRTH COLLIERY
W. Adie
J. Boyd
G. Boyle
P. Burnett
W. Carson
R. Clark
J. Cunningham
A. Flanagan
S. Fleming
I. Fox – Lumph
H. Howie
M. Hoggan
J. Hunter
T. Hynd
D. Jamieson
J. Lindsay
W. Kane
T. McGuire
J. McKenna
N. McLeod
T. McNeil
D. McQueen
J. McQueen
T. Mackie
D. Melville
G. Miller
W. Montgomery
S. Nelson
P. Park
W. Paterson
G. Robertson
T. Robertson
B. Ross
I. Ross.
R. Simpson
D. Sneddon
F. Somerville
J. Stein
J. Stewart
A. Strachan
B. Telford
J. Traynor
T. Traynor
D. Veale
G. Wooley

BOGSIDE COLLIERY
J. Banks
J. Elder
J. Reid
J. Reid Jnr.